The Headhunter's Granddaughter

Terry Iwanski

The Headhunter's Granddaughter
Copyright © 2023 by Terry Iwanski

Published in the United States of America

Library of Congress Control Number: 2024901086
ISBN   Paperback: 979-8-89091-408-8
ISBN   Hardback: 979-8-89091-409-5
ISBN   eBook: 979-8-89091-410-1

All rights reserved. No part of this publication may be reproduced, stored in a retrieval system or transmitted in any way by any means, electronic, mechanical, photocopy, recording or otherwise without the prior permission of the author except as provided by USA copyright law.

The opinions expressed by the author are not necessarily those of ReadersMagnet, LLC.

ReadersMagnet, LLC
10620 Treena Street, Suite 230 | San Diego, California, 92131 USA
1.619. 354. 2643 | www.readersmagnet.com

Book design copyright © 2023 by ReadersMagnet, LLC. All rights reserved.

Cover design by Jhiee Oraiz
Interior design by Don De Guzman

The Headhunter's Granddaughter
Based on the life of Pedo Rupa
Written by Terry Iwanski
Copyright 2023 Terry Iwanski

CHAPTER 1

My Loving Grandfather

I don't remember anything about my early childhood. Only what my grandfather, the headhunter, had told me. I do not remember his birth name because no one used proper names in the jungle. You were either an auntie or an uncle, a brother or a sister, a cousin, and so forth. So, Grandfather once said to me, "You were born sometime in November of 1959." He didn't remember the exact day. In the jungles of Borneo, dates like names were of little importance. He didn't even know the year he was born. My guess would have been around 1923.

Grandfather told me I was one of ten children born to his son, Tungan. Two others had died at birth in their small bamboo and sage leaf hut. Some of the older children would sleep outside at night beside the cooking fire. I was put in a sling basket which hung from a rafter. My mother would push the basket back and forth to put me to sleep. It made a creaking sound that would lull me to sleep.

Our hut was in the village named Kampong Gerung some twenty-five miles from the nearest town. There weren't any roads, only foot trails through the dense green jungle.

Soon after I was born, my mother and father decided to give me away because they already had too many mouths to feed. And my father had an unmarried brother who needed someone to work and cook for him. But he would have to wait until I grew older.

I had to be breastfed by the village women who passed me around many times. My uncle, whose name was Ganot, didn't know how to handle me. However, my grandfather, who lived in the same hut, felt connected to me and watched over me like a father. He once said, "Finding milk donors in the middle of the night was the hardest thing he did since the new mothers had their babies to feed." He said, "I would often end up crying myself to sleep at night," which unfortunately kept my uncle awake. Because he had such a short temper, he would quickly become angry and, as time went on, he would take out his anger on me.

Around six months, the village women grew tired of feeding me, so they told my grandfather to spoon-feed me with rice and soft vegetables.

One night, while he was feeding me by the fire, I kept staring at the bright moon between spoonfuls of rice. And the thought came to him that I didn't, as yet, have a name. He named me 'Pedo,' which means "I see the moon," in jungle language. At last, I was somebody.

I soon grew to be a toddler, and as yet, did not have diapers or outside clothes, as did the other children. Potty training had never been a priority, so grandfather just hoped I would be outside whenever 'nature' called. I would often pee down my leg for months until I learned how to squat. One night, while standing next to the fire, I tripped 'butt-first' and fell into the embers. My brother, Nipor, who had come for a visit, quickly pulled me from the flames. A large scar, to this day, remains on the left side of my bottom. When I notice it now, I think of that night and wish I had lived with my whole family, like the other children in our village. It made me feel empty, angry, and sad. But, of course, I always had my grandfather, the staple of my early life.

After the fire incident, a nice village woman took pity on me for being naked all of the time. She gave me an oversized white hand-me-down cotton smock, which I would wear night and day. I would only take it off to wash it in the waterfall near our hut. I would also bathe myself in the frigid mountain water.

When I turned six, my grandfather sent me to the village's primary school, which was a very long walk to and from our home. The teacher taught us the basics and some English and Bahasa, the national dialect, which is different from my jungle dialect. I had fun at school but was shy, partly because I only had a stub of a pencil with which to write and no eraser. I had to wet my finger to wipe out any mistakes.

But the most embarrassing 'omission' during my first year at school was not having any underwear. During exercise class, while doing jumping jacks, the other children could see my private parts! They would point at me and laugh.

One day, my grandfather met me after class, which surprised me since he had never done that before. He then took me to the village communal hut to show me several human skulls hanging from the ceiling; there were many. He told me how the Japanese had invaded Borneo during WWII to seize natives for slave labor. I didn't know anything about the Japanese or the war. But I could see the pride in his face when he pointed to four of those white skulls, which he said he had taken during the war. When my uncle found out about what he had done, he said I would stop wasting time with my grandfather and school. Instead, I needed to work more. I was already cooking, cleaning, and gathering firewood. He told me it was time to start helping him tap rubber trees deep into the jungle, which scared me. When my grandfather protested, my uncle struck him hard on his right arm with a club, which remained paralyzed for the rest of his life. At times, my uncle proved to be a cruel and vicious man. He never once said a kind word to me, nor did he ever smile.

Perhaps he was jealous of the bond grandfather, and I had come to feel towards one another. So, my education slowly came to a stop. But I did manage to make it through the sixth grade, even under protest from my uncle. When I argued with him about it, his anger toward me became even more intense. Cleary, I was beginning to get a mind of my own. But it didn't matter to my uncle. I was still wearing the same worn-out cotton smock. And I was yet to be given any underwear or shoes. At the time, I was ten years old and growing fast.

Due to the small size of the hut, I shared a sago leaf mat with my grandfather at night. I felt safe and warm beside him. And one night, he fell into a deep sea of dreams as he tossed and turned, making terrifying sounds as if he were in the middle of a nightmare.

I woke him and said, "Grandfather, what is wrong?"

As he opened his eyes, I could see the sweat dripping down his face. That night he told me the story of what had happened to him so many years ago during the war. And, in my own words, this is what I remember him telling me:

"Grandfather pushed his hut's bamboo door open into December of 1943, two years after the bombing of Pearl Harbor, and he had his machete in hand, muscles tensed, and beads of sweat covered his tattooed body. The twenty-two-year-old man stopped, spit on the ground, then excused himself to the jungle ghosts. He reached under his loincloth, grabbed himself, and peed.

The morning was misty. Grandfather could see it dressing the palm trees in layers, soon to stand naked in the sun. The scent of the air, however, was different to him somehow, so he raised his chin and inhaled deeply. In some strange way, the air smelled 'yellow' to him. Looking down into the village, he saw the source of the smell. Two Japanese soldiers were jabbing hut doors with their bayonets, and shouting words that were meaningless to him. All he could think, was this was not right. These foreigners were invading his space. The villagers were in a panic as the women and children were running to hide in the jungle. A few brave natives stood their ground, spears in hand.

The Japanese soldiers confronted the small group of men, shouting unrecognizable words to them. Grandfather came down from his hut and stood behind the screaming soldiers. With two quick swipes from his machete, he slit each man's spine open; the men fell to the ground. The other men dragged their bodies off into the jungle, where he hacked off their heads, sticking them on planted spears. He then bent down and picked up the soldiers' helmets, placing them upon their heads. He smiled.

They left their bodies in place on the moist green jungle floor, soon to rot. The soldiers' heads and eyes seemed to be looking down at their headless bodies in surprise. Within a few hours, their face skin dried, pulling their eyelids back into their skulls, giving off an eerie wide-open stare. Their mouths fell open, revealing stained black teeth with a green, frothy drool, dripping down from the sides of their mouths.

The village children were afraid to look at these severed heads, but did, anyway. Then at night, each child slept close to their mothers, fearful of what they had seen. Within a few days, the jungle did its job, disposing of the flesh, eyes, and hair. The skulls were then hung in the communal hut for all to see. And the soldiers' helmets were used by the village women as cooking pots. At last, the jungle wove a coffin of green over each headless skeleton, as if these men were finally allowed 'to rest in peace.'

Grandfather asked the villagers for information about where the soldiers came from, but no one knew. Their village was planted deep inside Borneo, so news of anything 'outside' was remote to them. What bothered him the most was not knowing why these people were invading his space. He didn't like it.

The only thing he knew for sure was that the soldiers must have come from the coast. And the closest coastline was off the South China Sea. Now he was on the hunt looking for answers. Raising his chin again into the air, he took a deep breath for the scent of sea salt. Finding his direction, Grandfather grabbed his machete, slipped it into the waistband of his loincloth, turned, and nodded goodbye to the villagers. And within a few steps, he put himself into the maze of the jungle.

He was not afraid. Everything he needed for survival was within arm's reach. He would travel for days following his nose, cutting and slashing his way toward the coast, determined to find an answer. Then, the salt scent became tinted with that strange smell of 'yellow' he had first sensed back in the village. There was also a tinge of sweetness that made his manhood tingle. He was getting close to something.

The jungle cleared, and he found the source of his stimuli. Below, he spied a massive compound of buildings surrounded by barbed wire fencing and guard towers. Just outside the enclosure were several rice paddies with semi-naked white women tending to them. Some were breastfeeding babies as they worked. Japanese guards slowly walked around the paddies, rifles shouldered.

Unknown to grandfather, he was at the Batu Lintag prison camp for women. All he knew was, "This is not right." His testosterone surged mixing with the estrogen and pungent smell of 'yellow' that floated in the air. Filled with anger and lust, he grabbed his machete, screamed in rage, then attacked the soldiers.

"Wake up, grandfather! You're having a bad dream," I yelled as I pushed on his arm. "Wake up! Please." He woke and went outside to pee. He then made jungle coffee over an open fire for himself and me.

The bond between us became more durable over the years. I would often go with him deep into the lush jungle to gather food. The green vegetables were easy to pick because they were low to the ground and plentiful. The fruit, on the other hand, was challenging. Rambutan, a red and green fruit, was fairly easy to pick because some of the trees they grew on were not very tall. But not much to eat because the brown seed took up most of the room inside.

The best tasting but the hardest fruit to get was the Durian. It grew on large trees, too hard to climb. It was the size of a mishappened volleyball. The skin was brownish-green with the texture and looks of a bloated Horny Toad. When cut open, it had a powerful sweet odor, which some people found to be repugnant. The only way to get the Durian was to wait until it fell from the tree. So, Grandfather and I would build a small bamboo hut next to the tree and wait. It would often take days, but I would always bring rice to eat with what we gathered from the jungle. On occasion, I would spear a frog or catch a fish from the stream with a woven bamboo trap which my grandfather had made. We cooked the fish over the campfire, and the smoke from the damp wood would keep the mosquitoes at bay.

Then there were the snakes, big ones, eight-foot-long and as round as my eleven-year-old waist. They were large enough to swallow me whole. Their skin was multi-colored, to blend in with the jungle. And there were small snakes that were thin like baby bamboo sprouts. They were the most dangerous because of their speed and lethal bite. I, however, was not afraid of them.

One night as we sat in front of our hut, there was a shimmer in the grass. It danced in tune with the flickering fire. And there it was. The biggest snake I had ever seen. Its belly was swelled double its size as the snake slithered slowly in the grass. Grandfather took his spear, carefully approached the large serpent, and with one quick thrust, staked its head to the ground. But the snake's smooth, shiny body refused to die. We could hear it twist and turn throughout the night. In the morning, it was still.

There was no time to waste. The jungle was turning up the heat. Grandfather and I had to skin the snake before its meat turned rancid. Using some vine as a rope, grandfather hung it from a tree. He took his machete and, with one quick swing, cut the head off. The blood drained out and, he caught some in a coconut shell, drinking it for 'virility.' He offered me some, but I said, "No."

As we peeled the skin down, the white meat glistened like a pearl. Then came the big bump in the stomach. Grandfather slit it open. Out fell a partially digested monkey, which was no surprise to us, as monkeys were an everyday snack. But I was fond of them, so I buried the monkey and made a bamboo cross, tied with green reed. Now it was time to work; we cut the snake into pieces to share with the village people.

Grandfather and I stayed in the village for two days to reap the benefits of the snake. We didn't have to cook for ourselves. The women were more than happy to do the job. They would take a long knife, cut and sliver green bamboo into skewers, pierce the snake bits, salt them, and roast them over the open fire. No fat would drip out, as it did with the brown wild boar meat. The pearly snake was lean.

On the other hand, the men didn't have to hunt, leaving them more time to drink jungle-made rice wine, tasting like kerosene. They were good at drinking it, and it always came before work, food, or sex. All in all, the men didn't do much beside hunting. The women did most of the work at home, and in the rice paddies. They were passive to the men. Even at my young age, I noticed that passivity in these women. I didn't quite understand it but unconsciously filed the information away in my mind for future use.

It was now time to go back to the jungle hut and wait for the durian fruit to drop. We got a late start. It was dark by the time we got back to our small 'make-shift' hut. I started a fire while looking around for big snakes, thinking to myself I could have easily been that monkey. The snake could have slithered into our hut, and as he coiled around me in my sleep, I would wake to hear my bones snapping just before I stopped breathing.

That night I stayed by the fire. There was no reason to leave it because we had gathered plenty of firewood. But I had to pee. As I walked away from the fire, a canopy of stars appeared in the darkness overhead. Like the stars above us, the light from fireflies helped to punctuate the stillness of the night.

I took heed of the sounds that came from the jungle, some known, some not. If I got too close to the edge of darkness, the skin on my arms and legs would get goosebumps, and I could feel my heart thump, thump, thump. I peed, then quickly returned to the fire and the safety of my grandfather.

During the evenings, my grandfather would tell me stories of early Borneo. One story was about a man from the village who had a young son. The boy wanted to go with his father, who was going to slash and burn part of the jungle to grow vegetables. Knowing this could be dangerous, the father told his son he could not go, but the boy insisted with tears running down his face, so his father gave in. Trying to keep him safe from the fire, he tied him in the top of a palm tree, so he would not fall out, and, at the same time, he could watch his father work. Thinking the flames would not touch the boy, his father carefully set the fire. As he cut and burned away at the jungle, the father would call out, every now and then, to see if his son was okay. The boy would answer. Then he called out again, but the only sound he heard was the crackling and popping of the fire's flames. The father rushed in the direction of his son. The thick smoke was stifling. He arrived to find his son still secured high in the palm tree, but the young boy had died, suffocated by the smoke, and sadly burned on his legs.

But this time with my grandfather, having fun in the jungle was over. It lasted only a few days. And we both knew uncle would be furious when we got back to the hut. He was. He told my grandfather to keep away from me. As far as he was concerned, I was his property! From now, I would be working for him and helping him to tap rubber trees. For some reason, grandfather was afraid of him, and from then on, he kept away from me during the day.

When my uncle banned me from my grandfather, his health started to decline because I would make him special food that was easy to chew. His teeth were in such bad condition he had difficulty eating.

Then things got worse. My uncle would force him to stay in our hut while we worked in the jungle during the day by putting a lock outside the door.

I asked him, "Why?" My uncle said, "He is bothering other villagers for food, which is embarrassing. But at night, Grandfather and I still shared our mat, and I still enjoyed his warmth, kindness, and love.

CHAPTER 2

"You are mine, not theirs!"

The roosters hadn't even crowed yet; it was that early in the morning when I felt his heavy presence pushing down upon me. I slowly opened my eyes and saw my uncle squatting beside me, his eyes fixed in a menacing glare upon mine. It scared me so profoundly I wet myself. I kept silent as he spoke to me in a slow, quiet growl, "You should be up by now. Time for work!"

Grandfather awoke, too, but didn't move or speak. I then stirred our cooking fire, adding twigs and a few more substantial pieces of wood, as the brightness and warmth of its glowing embers pushed the heavy morning mist aside.

There wasn't any time for breakfast because the rubber trees would get 'stingy' with their white milk sap if it got too late into the morning. My uncle was now my taskmaster. He snarled, "Follow me," as we quickly made our way into the jungle. It was still dark, but he knew where we were going, so I hastened to keep up, plodding along in the darkness. His feet were heavily calloused after many years of walking barefooted over this rough terrain. He never wore any shoes. So he moved quicker than me, as I struggled to keep up with him.

My feet were not yet strong enough to resist the thorns and brambles that covered the jungle floor. I would often fall back, and when this happened, uncle would stop, turn around and growl, "Hurry up, you lazy good for nothing!" But walking far behind him would one day be to my benefit, unknown to me at the time.

When we arrived at the rubber tree site, the sun was glaring down upon us. My uncle gave me a knife and a bucket into which I would collect the slurpy white milk. At first, he spoke sternly, "Listen to me! This a difficult task," but I caught on fast. I was bright, even at the age of eleven. At times he would scold me for some minor mishap, but it was clear to me that I was smarter than he though. Unlike my uncle, I had some schooling, whereas he could neither read nor write.

We did this for endless months, and the same routine would repeat itself, day in and day out. I cooked, cleaned, tapped rubber, and cared for my grandfather and uncle. And still, I had to wear the same white cotton smock every day, with no underwear or shoes.

One day after tapping rubber, I squatted in front of our hut, sharpening my knife on my uncle's honing stone. Without warning, he came up behind me, grabbed the 'stone' from my hand, and struck me hard on my head's right side. I fell to the ground in pain, holding my hand over my ear. Then, my uncle walked away, without any explanation, with the honing stone still in his hand. My uncle did not have much of anything, but this was his honing stone. And he wanted me to know it was his. From that day on, I was deaf in my right ear because my uncle had broken my eardrum. I remember feeling hurt, betrayed, and angry. It was time for a change. But no one seemed to care about me--even my own parents.

Soon after that terrible incident, my parents and siblings moved twelve miles away to my oldest sister's husband's big stilt house, whose name was Embrose. They moved there to help tend a rice paddy not far from their new home. Their absence didn't bother me that much because I was already banned from their house anyway. If I dared to walk by their home, I would be shooed away like a stray dog.

But at least they left my six-year-old brother, Doros, with my mother's sister, Sambat, so that he could attend school. At last, I had a small part of my family nearby. We would goof around when our uncle was away selling the rubber we tapped. He would be gone for at least two days because he walked twenty-five miles to Kuching. I enjoyed myself when my uncle was away because I could breathe freely and not feel overshadowed by his uncontrolled wrath. Doros and I would make slingshots from tree branches and use bicycle tubes for the elastic part. We would go out into the jungle, hunt small birds of many colors, and shoot them down. Afterward, we would pluck their feathers, build a small fire, roast them, and have our own private feast.

One night when my uncle was away, my grandfather told me another story; it would be his last. And I have treasured this tale all my life.

We were sitting by the cooking fire when I asked him to tell me about himself as a young man. He nodded, put his hand on his chin, closed his eyes, and I could tell he was thinking. Then, turning to me, his eyes sparkled from the fire. Grandfather smiled and started talking:

"I had a simple life until one morning, I saw three 'far-off' dancing points of light coming from the jungle foliage. As the lights came closer, I could see it was the sun's glaring reflection upon metal objects hanging around three white people's necks. I blinked the 'objects' into focus; they were heavy silver crosses hung from leather strings.

Standing before me were two middle-aged men and one woman dressed in white long-sleeved blouses and tan slacks. They had heavy backpacks and were sweating profusely. I had never seen or smelled white people before. They had an odor of conceit, an excessive appreciation of their virtue. The woman fixed her cold gray eyes on my loincloth. The men took off their backpacks and helped with hers, breaking her stare. They were missionaries, determined to save me and the village from our arrogant and ignorant selves. Communication was labored. The woman spoke 'Bahasa,' Malaysia's national language, a jigsaw of words with the jungle dialect. The two men went around handing out little black Bibles to my friends, which meant nothing to them because they were in English. None of the village people could read or write.

The woman still focused on my loincloth, wanting to get me into pants. She dug into her backpack and brought out a pair of tan shorts. Then she hand-gestured for me to put them on. I just stood there, so she impatiently tugged at the corners of my loincloth with her hands. It fell to the ground, exposing my brown penis. She turned her head in disdain.

One of the male missionaries saw her distress, came over, and helped me into the shorts and then a red T-shirt with a pocket. I felt trapped in these clothes, no longer able to feel the jungle's warm moist breath upon my skin.

I needed to get away, turn, and run to the safety of the jungle. After finding my comfort spot, I sat down and explored the shorts pocket, finding a folding knife, which was new to me because I only knew of machetes.

Wanting more time alone, away from the missionaries' overpowering assault, I stayed in the jungle for three days and nights. To fill my time, I chopped down a small green bamboo stem and 'whittled' out six hand flutes for the village children. My father had taught me how to make them, but I had, until now, always used a machete. The small knife was much handier.

After the third day, I walked back to the village with the flutes, ready to hand them out. The children swarmed me. Used to seeing the women with exposed brown breasts, I was surprised that the missionaries had now covered them with white, ill-fitting bras. Many of the women tugged at their straps.

I had had enough and confronted the missionaries by removing my shorts and T-shirt. I glanced at the women to follow my lead. After they released their bras, the missionaries left our village, tight-fisted and tight-jawed.

The children tried to play their flutes into the night, but their shrill toneless noise clashed with the natural harmony of the jungle's symphony of sound. After a while, the children fell silent and let the jungle music lull them to sleep."

My grandfather's missionary story has stuck with me over the years. Shortly after he shared it with me, I turned twelve but remained as unhappy as ever. In the interim, things were beginning to change. The villagers helped surveyors build a rough white rock road to Kuching. And the city of Kuching had an old beat-up green and yellow bus that would arrive early every morning and return later that evening for people wanting to shop or trade. This bus would pass right by Embrose's house, where my parents lived, which gave me options, which I needed, because things began to worsen with my uncle.

Walking back from the jungle one day, after tapping rubber from the trees, I felt a warm sensation that seemed to be running down between my legs. Thinking I must have cut myself on a branch, I reached down to discover the source. It was blood coming from the center of me. I panicked and tried to stop the blood flow with the palm of my hand; it didn't stop. My uncle was walking a few yards in front of me, and I thought perhaps I should ask him what was happening to me.

I didn't. I would rather have died first than to ask my uncle for help. The bleeding stopped four days later of its own accord.

I soon discovered what had happened to me. A few months earlier, I had befriended an older village girl by the name of Putri. I shyly asked her about the bleeding, and she smiled. She told me it was a normal thing that happened to all young girls. According to her, it was the body's way of preparing them for motherhood. Surprisingly, Putri gave me my first pair of underwear to use when that time of the month came once again. She also told me to use clean rags to absorb the blood, rather than having it drip down between my legs.

However, I was still going through a wide range of emotions, mostly anger and sadness, hostility toward my uncle, and sadness for not having my mother beside me to help me grow up. It was time for me to start making plans to get back together with my mother. But I needed money. So, I started saving scraps of rubber that I had scraped from my tapping bucket. Of course, I needed to keep this a secret from my uncle. After a few weeks, I had enough to sell to a man in the village. I got twenty-five cents, which was enough for a bus ride to my mother and father's house.

At the time, my thinking was that if I just showed up, they would see what they had given away and take me back with love, hugs, and kisses. So, I waited until my uncle was busy cutting down a palm tree behind our hut, and I boarded the morning bus to Kuching. As we neared my parent's house, I told the driver to stop, and I got off.

I was so excited to see them and be welcomed with open arms that I started to cry happy tears of joy. But my tears soon dried. My parents met me with blank stares that said, "Why are you here?" My heart sank into the pit of my stomach; My parents' somber greeting was not what I expected

But it got worse when my uncle found out. He came and brought me back on the evening bus. Uncle dragged me out of their house, kicking and screaming. He yelled back at me, "You are mine, not theirs." And then he pushed me into the bus, while people on the bus stared at us in silence.

The next few weeks were horrible. My uncle watched me like a hawk. Even when I talked with my grandfather, he would try to listen in, thinking we were dreaming up another escape plan for me. My grandfather remained passive, afraid of my uncle and what he might do. I, however, was not.

Then one day, still barefooted while working in the jungle, I stepped on some thorns and severely cut my feet. I dropped to my knees in pain. As I looked up, an airliner passed over the jungle canopy above. I thought to myself, "Someday, I will be on that airplane!"

My uncle had caught on to my selling the rubber scraps from my bucket, so I no longer had a way of making any money for bus fare. So, I went to my friend Putri for help, and between the two of us, we devised a plan for my escape. Putri was a babysitter in Kuching, and she had learned of a Chinese family who needed a babysitter. But first, I had to get on the morning bus without my uncle becoming aware of our plan.

I also needed to acquire suitable clothes and a pair of shoes to take with me. Later that evening I met with Putri, who gave me a small bundle of clothes, but no shoes. I hid the bundle by the side of the road a reasonable distance from the village. In the morning, Putri would board the bus first, and then she would tell the driver to stop and pick me up.

That night I tried to sleep but was so nervous, my eyes would not close. The next morning before dawn, my uncle and I went to work in the jungle, our daily routine. I followed him, and his pace, as always, was faster than mine. Deliberately, I kept walking slower and slower until my uncle was far ahead of me, nearly out of sight. I was terrified that he would turn around to check on me, but he didn't. Finally, I stopped in my tracks, my heart beating like a small drum. I turned around quickly and ran back to our hut, placing my knife and bucket neatly beside the door. I walked into our hut. My grandfather was still asleep. As I gently kissed him goodbye, he remained sleeping. Sadly, I would never see him again.

I ran as fast as I could to where I had hidden my clothes. As I pulled the bundle from the bushes, I heard the old bus coming down the road with a rattle and roar. It stopped as we had planned, and Putri standing in the doorway, extended her hand and helped me inside. She gave the bus driver my fare, and off we went.

The bus was nearly full, and only two seats remained, apart from each other. I sat down beside an older man who began to make small talk. Turning toward me with a smile, he carefully slid his hand onto my leg, which I did not expect. I stood up quickly in the aisle and grabbed the rope strap hold, which dangled over my head. At the innocent age of twelve, I was beginning to blossom, but I was far more concerned about my survival. The bus finally stopped in the small town of Kuching, near the coast. Before getting off, Putri gave me one final gift, a used pair of flip-flops.

We started walking towards the Chinese lady's house. My flip-flops felt strange on my feet as they spanked my calloused heels. They seemed to be saying to me, "You're free. You're free!"

CHAPTER 3

"Aling"

It was just a three-block walk from the bus stop to the Chinese lady's house. Those blocks felt like miles. With each step I took, my feet got heavier and heavier, and my mouth turned dry. I was nervous.

When we reached the house, Putri knocked on the door. It opened, and there stood a tall, nice-looking woman. She was wearing a colorful silk sarong, and behind her, holding on to her leg was a cute little girl. The lady smiled, and my friend spoke first, saying in Bahasa, "Here is your babysitter, as I promised." Then Putri gently pushed my hand towards the lady for a handshake. As we shook, I glanced at the lady's face with a nervous smile. I was lucky I knew how to speak Bahasa. I said, "Hello." And the Chinese lady returned the greeting, "Hello," in Bahasa. She was bilingual.

Then Putri talked to the lady about my wages. I didn't know how much I'd earn because no one had ever paid me for anything. They struck a deal for twenty-five Ringgits per month, about six U.S. dollars. When I heard this, I felt rich for the first time. My friend then smiled at the lady and me, and then she turned and walked away. I never saw Putri again to thank her for helping me. I would later learn that she took a job in Singapore, working for a wealthy Chinese family. I was sure she was doing well and on her way toward a good life.

It was now time for me to work. First, the lady told me to address her as Meiling. She then showed me around the house, which was huge compared to my uncle's hut. It had concrete floors with throw rugs in all four rooms. She had to show me how to use an indoor toilet and a shower. Then Meiling took me into the baby's room, where I would sleep on the floor. She then outlined the duties she expected from me, including cleaning, cooking, and taking care of the baby, and two other preschool-aged girls, who also had beds in the same room.

Meiling didn't mother me, as I was only an employee. But she was kind to me and even bought me some clothes, underwear, and a brand-new pair of yellow flip-flops. For the first time in my life, someone other than my grandfather, with his loving ways, made me feel special.

The first night I was scared since it was a lot of responsibility for a twelve-year-old girl to undertake. The baby slept in a sling basket, which creaked back and forth as it moved. The sound comforted not only the baby but also helped me to fall asleep. The next day began at 4:00 AM when the baby woke up crying. Her mother showed me how to make a warm bottle for her and clean the baby's diaper. I did lots of 'poopy' diaper washing in a small bucket with warm soapy water, then hung them up outside to dry on a clothesline. The two other girls were easy to take care of because they were older. I would mainly cook for them, do their laundry, and sometimes play with them in between my chores.

When Meiling's husband came home after work, I would have the rice ready for dinner. Meiling would stir-fry vegetables and sometimes add bits of meat or fish. I would serve the family first, then after the family finished their meal, I would clean the plates and table. Then it would be my turn to eat.

Meiling's husband was tall and lean and worked somewhere in Kuching. He spoke only Chinese to his wife and children and also to me. Because of this, I learned to speak Chinese during the time I lived with them. I became aware that I was very good at learning different languages. The only downside to the job was never having a day off and rarely having any free time to leave the house. Also, I noticed there was an undercurrent of class distinction. I was only a 'Bidayuh,' a jungle girl to them. And they were Chinese, a cut or two above everybody else, according to them.

I was now fifteen, and my feet were itching to move on. I found another job with an Indian family not far from Meiling's house by asking around. When I told her I was leaving, she said, "That's okay." Her children were now getting older, and they could more or less take care of themselves. Meiling expressed no emotion when I told her I would be leaving. Nor did I. But the children cried when I told them I was going as if they were losing a close friend. Which I suppose I was to them in the end. And I remember a tear beginning to form in my eye when I said goodbye to them in Chinese.

I went straight away to my new job with the Indian family. Nadia was the mother of twin girls and three boys, all pre-adolescent in age but friendly, obedient, and well-mannered. Nadia and her husband were school teachers and needed help because both worked all day at their jobs. Nadia, like Meiling, also spoke Bahasa and her native language of Hindi. I learned to speak some Hindi, but my head was getting too full because I knew my jungle dialect, Bahasa, Chinese, and a little English.

My workdays were the same as when I was with the last family, with the same chores: cooking, cleaning, laundry, and childcare. But now, I was making more money than when I was with the Chinese family. And another plus; I now had a room and a bed all to myself. My first real bed, and for the first time, some absolute privacy! Over time Nadia and I developed a warm friendship, and on some weekends, she would take me to see Hindi movies. Another first, I had never been inside a movie house before. It was great!

But after living with them for about three years, they no longer needed me because their children had grown enough to take care of themselves, for the most part. I was nineteen now, had needs of my own, and my hormones were beginning to rage. I had had enough of small children, the noise, their crying, and their poopy diapers.

Then, one day Nadia asked me if I would be willing to do her a favor. She wanted me to help an older Indian couple who had recently taken on two baby girls' care. The couple was beyond the age of having children themselves and needed help. They had become the two babies' guardians to help out a single mother of a close friend. Nadia wanted me to be their teacher. Without hesitation, I said, "Yes."

The first photo ever taken of Pedo after she got a job in Kuching.

The couple ran a small business from their house and acquired a rotary telephone, another first for me. Sometimes I would answer it when they were gone. I thought it was a clever device and came to enjoy using it. But I didn't have anyone to call. My family would not get a telephone until more than twenty years later.

After six months, I had taught the elderly couple all I knew about raising babies, and I was eager to get on with my life. I had enough money in my purse and a burning desire to get on with my life, which I did. No longer needed by the Indian family or the elderly couple, I rented a one-room apartment in a stilt-house building in downtown Kuching. The place had sparse furniture, along with a communal shower and toilet.

I found a job in a street cafe that served chicken, rice, coffee, tea, and Coke. No menu needed. That is where I befriended a fellow employee, whose name was Somoy. Her job was serving the drinks, and my job was serving chicken rice. Being of like ages and minds, Somoy moved in with me and shared the rent.

After work in the evenings, we would walk a short distance and sit on the curb in front of a movie house, only to watch the boys pass by. I was in full bloom and would enhance my beauty by wearing short skirts, tight blouses, and bright colors, which attracted the boys. The only problem was Somoy. She was jealous of my charms, and she was also short-tempered. Fueled by an abundance of hormones, she jumped a prostitute that favored the same area we were occupying, saying to her, "Get out of here! This movie house is our place, not yours to spoil."

The fight was on. I jumped in to pull hair, kick, scratch, and scream. The police soon arrived to stop the struggle and take everyone into custody, uncuffed. The police detained the prostitute at the station since they had dealt with her before. Somoy and I were set free and reclaimed our spot in front of the theater. But deep down inside, I was sad. I felt this might become the doorstep for the rest of my life.

Then the bottom dropped out with another incident, which saddened me even further. The one constant in my life died, my grandfather. I heard the news through word of mouth, no phone, just airspace. I asked my boss for time off to return to the village and say goodbye.

He said, No! you have to work. I thought to myself, *What a bastard*. Several months later, I made it back to the village and, with help, found the spot in the jungle where his funeral pyre had been. The jungle had knitted a lush green blanket over his gravesite. I spoke to my grandfather in our jungle language, cried, and sadly walked away.

As I had hoped, my life would change while sitting in front of the movie house one evening. Somoy and I were at our spot on the curb when two Chinese guys walked by us. One stopped to talk with me. The other smiled at Somoy but went on into the theater. I was nervous, never having had much to do with boys, only work. Unknown to me, those few short words of exchange would seal my fate.

Somoy, at last, had met someone she liked, and within a few months, they were married. She moved out of the stilt rooming house, leaving me alone to sit on the curbside in front of the movie house. Then, out of the blue, the Chinese boy I had met earlier came back to the theater to find me one day. We sat and talked, making plans to see each other again. His smooth charms and good looks took me quite by surprise. His name was Hee Ping, and as time passed, he filled the void in my otherwise lonely life.

Our relationship would grow as we dug into each other's passions. Being no beginner, he took my virginity with lust and force. I was scared and tight, which seemed only to excite him more. He forced his way in, and I was in pain. He did not fully enter me but exploded and then pulled out. Then, as nature would have it, Hee Ping planted his seed in my fertile virginal body; and it began to grow. I was afraid and uncertain, not being married and having little money.

Planning for my future, I rented a four-room apartment without Hee Ping's help. I knew I had to take control because he was not there for the most part. He would come and go as he pleased just for sex. Once again, I was on my own. Nine months later, the planted seed flowered. And on May 20th, 1981, I was alone in my apartment and went into the bathroom to pee. Water gushed out from between my legs. I was scared and didn't know what was happening. So, I asked my neighbor, who was a nurse. She said my "water broke," and the baby was soon to come. She called for an ambulance. I asked if I could use her phone to contact Hee Ping's friend to let him know where I was going. He said he would find him and relay the message.

When I got to the hospital, I had to register and show my national ID card, which had my full name, Pedo AK Rupa. But I went by 'Harina' because it was then a 'fad' to pick a Christian first name.

I was in painful labor for several hours, then, in the middle of the night, my baby girl Aling was born. Hee Ping never showed up.

I couldn't work for a few days after getting out of the hospital. I was very sore. It was then that Hee Ping finally showed up looking guilty; he gave me some money. I asked him why he hadn't come to the hospital, and he said, "I did, but they said no one by the name of Harina had registered there that afternoon. I asked him why he didn't ask for Rupa? He said, "I forgot your last name." I thought to myself,

"What a shallow man, let alone our 'shallow' relationship. I vowed never to let any man hurt me like that ever again.

By the time Aling was eight months old, Hee Ping had disappeared. He had only held his daughter a few times. Hurt and anger now filled the empty spot in my belly. I moved from what I believed would be our apartment to a smaller apartment next to my sister's for emotional support. And I would wait for Hee Ping's return for months, which turned into years.

Knowing where his parents lived, I finally decided to seek him out. They resided in Sibu, one-hundred-and-fifteen miles downriver from Kuching, where they owned a wholesale business. So, with Aling in tow, I boarded a boat for Sibu. The trip took all day.

Aling and I walked hand in hand into their business office. There sat Hee Ping with his mother by his side. He stood up, shocked, yet held out his hand to Aling, who wanted nothing to do with him and cried. Then his mother chimed in, saying, "We don't want you and your child. You are a Bidayuh, a jungle girl. We are Chinese!" Again, that class distinction had entered my life. Hee Ping rented a hotel room for his daughter and me for the night. The next day we returned to Kuching.

I was livid; I told him I wanted his driver's license to prove our child's existence. He gave it to me but only in defiance, as he reached for the phone in the room and dialed his Chinese girlfriend.

He said to her, "I will be late, sweetheart. Something has come up." He broke my heart as he continued to talk with her. I felt like he had kicked me in the gut, and I could not breathe. And yet, the warm innocence of first love felt safe within me. No one could take that away, ever.

During the long trip back up the river to Kuching, the current of my emotions eddied deep. I was absorbed in my pain but had to be strong because of my daughter.

For the next few years, my focus would be on raising Aling. Going back to work at the chicken rice cafe meant I would have to commute by city bus because of my last apartment move. There was no more sitting in front of the movie house anymore, watching life go by; Hee Ping had sucked me into it, then left me to drown on my own.

Pedo's next-door neighbor was Aling's babysitter while she worked at a restaurant in Kuching.

I desperately needed somebody to watch Aling while I worked. At times I would leave her with an older man who lived next door. He was a gentleman and reminded me of my grandfather. I trusted him. On some days, I would have to take her to work and park her in an unoccupied dining room.

As Aling reached school age, I knew I had to enroll her. I sought my parents' help, even though they lived some twenty miles away. Part of this decision came when I decided that Aling would go to the same school as me when I was a child. It was a suitable arrangement, and this went on for years. I, in return, would help my parents with food and clothes; they, too needed help.

Aling was happy to have a surrogate mother and father. She would get much one on one attention because they were alone now since all their children were grown.

As I did with my grandfather, Aling would sleep with her grandmother on the same mat as a child. Grandmother would playfully pinch her budding breast nipples to wake her in the morning to get ready for school, while her grandfather would boil coffee over an open wood fire.

Aling did well in school and studied hard at night by the light from a handmade kerosene lamp, even though she had to use her finger to dig out the soot that accumulated inside her nose. And unlike her mother, I ensured Aling had handmade cotton underwear and more than one pencil with an eraser.

I returned to the village once a month to bring money and food and say to my father, "You threw your best child away. Now, I support you!" He just smiled in reply. But I was happy with the trade-off with Aling. And she seemed content with the arrangement, too.

Looking to better myself, I enrolled in a hairdressing and beauty school called 'Anita's' while working full-time. I did well and got my diploma, landing a job in an upscale salon called Andy Chaps, named after the Chinese owner. Even though I was in my mid-twenties, the staff would call me 'Mommy' because I often cooked for them at work.

Above is the business card that Pedo first gave to Terry after they met.

But I was far from looking like a mother. I was beautiful, well-built, and very sexy. And I knew it! I chose to stay away from boys because it would not look good as a single mother, and I was afraid of what people might say.

I kept the boys at bay for a long time. But as Aling grew, so did my passions and my desire for a companion. However, I did not want to end up pregnant and alone.

Like Hee Ping, the boys around Kuching just wanted a part of me, and I knew if I let them have their way, they would leave the rest of me, as did Aling's father. I knew all about that game. So, looking abroad, I answered an ad for a pen pal in the *Borneo Post*, English section. The pen pal lived in Germany, and we exchanged letters, but communication was awkward between us since it was a second language on both sides. The man sent me a picture of himself and his three children. He was fat and also a widower. Clearly, he was looking for a live-in caregiver for himself and his children. The letters stopped abruptly on my end.

CHAPTER 4

Respect and Love, at last.

I still wanted to find a good man who was not from Kuching. Since the newspaper ad turned sour, I let my hormones get the best of me. After all, it had been seven years since I was with a man. But this time, no one would abandon me. I was going to be in charge of my body and my needs.

I met a Chinese man much younger than me in a shopping mall, and we started dating. But this time, I controlled both the sex and the relationship. I used him, and he reaped the benefits I had to offer--a fair trade-off. But I didn't want to get pregnant, so I made him use a condom. If he didn't have one when I needed him, I would make sure he pulled out before climaxing. He didn't like that, so it didn't happen often. Then, after a while, he drifted away from me. Perhaps I wore him out? Anyway, I had spent two years with this man, and it was time for a change.

By then, I was over thirty and needed more out of life than just sex. I wanted a mature relationship with a man that grew out of respect and love for one another. I met another Chinese man who was ten years older than me. He seemed to have his head in the right place.

I didn't fall in love with him, but I tried to leave my heart open. We dated for over a year, and the sex was good, and I thought we had something good going. But there was a catch.

I found out he was married. In Malaysia, it is okay to have more than one wife. But he hid the fact he already had two wives. It hurt my feelings that he lied to me, and my trust in him went out the door. Had I just found myself an older version of Hee Ping? It became clear that I had made another wrong choice, so once I found out he was married--to not just one, but two wives!--I quickly cut off the relationship, much to his dismay. Even so, he would still try to be with me and sometimes follow me around. I was a little afraid of him because he had a short temper.

Soon, it felt like my heart was closing the door to love.

My painful experience with him was so disappointing that I felt I was doomed to be alone.

I was working late one afternoon when a white guy walked past me as I stood in the Salon's doorway, looking for customers. He was nice-looking, so I asked him if he wanted a scalp massage. He replied, "No, thank you," in English, with a friendly smile. I could tell he was American by his voice because it was not like the British or Australian customers, with their heavy accents, who came into the Salon.

He was the first American I ever talked to, and I wished then that my English was better. He had broad shoulders and looked to be in good shape. I followed him with my eyes until he disappeared around the corner.

A few minutes later, he reappeared and walked towards me, looking somewhat shy. He stopped before me and asked, "Would you like to have coffee with me after you get off work?". I didn't know what he meant--whether "have coffee with me" was code for something or what. Being unsure, I was scared and said, "No."

He said, "Okay," and walked away, and he looked like he was feeling defeated, for sure.

Then, I thought, "A handsome American just asked me out." I turned to my co-workers and asked them, "What should I do?" They said, "Go and get him back here, and say, Yes!" He was almost out of sight, but I caught his attention and waved to him to return. I spoke first and told him, "I will not have coffee with you but you can walk me to the bus after work because the boys bother me."

He said, "Okay. What time should I come back?"

I said, "10:00 PM." He was right on time.

As we walked to the bus stop, my emotions were going crazy. I thought, "What if the Chinese man sees us? Might he become jealous and create a problem with his anger? But for some reason, I felt safe walking beside this man. We exchanged names. I said, "My name is Harina Rupa, and he said, "My name is Terry Iwanski," which I had difficulty pronouncing. At the bus stop, we shook hands, and as the bus pulled away, our eyes followed each other until the bus disappeared into the night. When I got home, I wondered if I would ever see him again.

The following day, right after we opened the salon, Terry stood outside. To my surprise, he had shown up. I asked him again if he would like a scalp massage, and this time he said, "Sure." I carefully washed his hair, then rubbed his scalp as best as I could. As I worked, I noticed Terry seemed a bit nervous and stiff. When I finished his massage, he asked me to join him for coffee again. Having walked to the bus and feeling safe with him, I said, "Yes, "I get off early this afternoon. Come back around 4:00 PM."

He said, "Sounds good to me." Terry then went up to the counter to pay for the massage, but, for some reason, he didn't leave me a tip. I thought to myself, "What did I do wrong? I thought all Americans were rich?" Later, when we got together after work, I asked him why? He said, "A waiter told me I'm not supposed to tip in cafes? So, I assumed the custom would be similar in a salon?" He frowned. "I should have asked." He looked embarrassed and said, "I'm sorry." I smiled, but I would joke with him afterward and tease him often about his blunder.

Terry took me by taxi to a Hilton Hotel restaurant. I'm sure he was trying to impress me, which he did. I had never been inside any of the higher-end places in my life. I didn't know what to order since the menu was in English. My reading skills were even less impressive than my speaking when deciphering English. And this time, I also felt a bit nervous. So, I told the waiter, "I would like a fruit plate with my coffee, one cream, and one sugar." Terry ordered a cheese sandwich and black coffee.

We struggled to come up with things to say to each other. I thought, "Perhaps we both felt out of place in the Hilton?" So, afterward, we went to a street cafe and ordered Cokes. I felt more comfortable, and it seemed Terry was more at ease. That was when I dug into my purse, pulled out a pack, and lit one up. I could see by Terry's eyes he was shocked because he didn't smoke or drink. I tried hiding the cigarette under the table, but the smoke still floated. I then dropped it on the ground and crushed it out.

Terry then told me that he had smoked and drunk for seventeen years but felt it was time to quit. However, stopping was not easy, which sparked a pleasant conversation. He was forty-three years old and divorced with two grown children, so he asked me if I was married. I confessed, "Yes, but told him it was a jungle marriage, and I was now single and, like him, had a child, a twelve-year-old daughter. I told him the girl's father had abandoned us when she was eight months old. Terry asked me what a jungle marriage was, and I said, "Not a real one. We were just together."

We talked until dark, and I discovered that Terry owned his auto body repair shop back in the States. And I told him I would like to have my own business someday. I could tell he was attracted to me, and I thought, "Well, what was there not to like about me? I was young, sexy, and beautiful."

But it was time for me to go home. We walked to a taxi stand, and that was when Terry asked me, "Would you like to travel to other countries with me?" I said, "I don't have a passport." And at the same time, I did not tell him whether or not I liked the idea. The next thing I knew, he handed me enough money to go and get a passport.

The taxi took us to my sister Poni's and her husband's apartment, where I lived. Terry asked if he could walk me to the door. I had to say, "No."

He seemed hurt, and I couldn't help that. I'd known him so briefly that I was too shy to tell him about one of the landlord's rules. Only two people were allowed in each apartment, and there was a strict rule against overnight visitors. I was afraid he might have thought I was living with a boyfriend.

Before I got out of the taxi, Terry said, "I'm leaving for Kota Kinabalu on the island's other end. Then I will be going back home to the United States." It had been a fast two days!

He then asked me if I would see him off in the morning.

I was more than a little taken aback by his question. Besides my lack of experience dealing with anyone from another part of the world, I was not expecting him--or anyone--to ask me to go to an airport. It was simply something so far removed from anything I had ever done. I had to think about what he was asking, what it might mean about our interactions these past couple of days, and what might happen if I accepted his invitation to "see him off," something I wasn't quite sure I understood.

But he seemed to be a gentle, kind soul, and the way he asked me was so earnest that he disarmed my natural suspicions about whether something bad might happen to me if I "saw him off." So after a few moments, with the taxi waiting to take him away, I finally said, "Yes, if you can pick me up at the salon." The following day as we made our way to the airport, we held hands. While waiting for his flight, we decided to sit down. As Terry started to take a seat, I stopped him to brush some light debris from the chair. "No, wait, please," I said. "You never know who was sitting here before you." Terry looked at me with kindness in his eyes. I could see that this simple gesture on my part touched him deeply. I had made him feel very special.

Then it was time for him to board his plane. He bent down and gave me a light kiss on my cheek, a very polite man. He was wet-eyed, and I could tell he didn't want to go. I, too, had an intense feeling of emotion from deep inside. I thought, "Perhaps this is the man for me."

Later that day, Terry had flowers sent to me when he arrived in Kota Kinabalu. Those were the first flowers I'd ever received in my life. This man, I felt, was not fooling around. He wanted to be with me for the long run. Maybe this was the guy I'd been waiting for all these years?

The above picture was taken in the mall at a Kentucky Fried Chicken restaurant below Andy Chap's Hair Salon.

CHAPTER 5

THE TEST OF TRUE LOVE.

In the morning, two days after Terry had left, the phone rang at the salon. My boss answered it and said, "It sounds like the American." He called for me to come to the phone, then gave it to me without expression.

I was surprised and couldn't think of anything to say, so I said, "Hello." Terry said, "Well, I made it back home, and right now, I'm working in my body shop. Anyway, I figured I'd take a break and try to give you a call." Back in the states, it was late at night because of the time difference. I had only been at work for a couple of hours.

He spoke enthusiastically, and I could tell he was still very interested in me. He asked me if I was working on getting my passport and said he would be happy to send me anything I thought I might like from America. I said, "I'm okay." My boss looked at me again, this time sternly, and I could tell he wasn't happy about taking a phone call in the middle of my work schedule. So, I said, "Terry, I have to get back to work." He said, "Okay. I understand. I'll call you again in a couple of days."

My coworkers smiled as I came back to join them. They laughed, teased me, and said, "Harina, this could be your chance to live in the United States and get a green card. Don't let this opportunity slip by you." Getting a coveted green card' was a dream for many of my friends.

Terry and I wrote back and forth, but my English writing skills were poor, so I had to have my friends help me. But we got into the routine of talking on the phone once a week. We set up a specific time, so I would know it was him calling, and I would pick up the phone before my boss got to it. Those were the best times. Our secret talks went on for two months. Then Terry called, saying he had saved enough money for two airline tickets and extra traveling around Asia. By this time, I had my passport. He asked me, "Will you go with me?"

I did not want to end up heartbroken as I had done with the others. So, I put Terry to the test and asked, "Will you marry me?" If he said, "No," then the deal was off. If he said, "Yes," I would know he was serious about me and our relationship. He said, "Yes," without any hesitation. And it was then that my heart once again began to open.

He sent me my ticket to Singapore, where we would meet. But he put the name Harina Rupa on the ticket since it was the only name he knew. My co-workers told me my name was not the same as the one I used on my ID card/passport, Pedo AK Rupa.

He would have to change the name on the ticket on his end. I called him from the salon since the boss was gone[. He told me to tear up that ticket, and he'd send a new one post haste.

Then, I told him my real name, Pedo, which he preferred. When I told him what it meant, I see the moon, he liked it even better. Since that day, he has always called me Pedo.

I took a taxi to the airport and told the driver I felt nervous about traveling by air. He joked and said, Don't worry, not too many planes crash, with a smile. I didn't smile back and took my travel bag from the backseat. His joke didn't seem funny to me, and I left him no tip to show him how unfunny I thought he was. Seeing his smile fade as he took the money for the fare was a little pleasure.

Kuching airport is small, so it was easy to find my gate and board my plane. Learning how to do this would be good practice for any flights I might take since I would be making many such trips. Terry arrived in Singapore a day early to make sure he would be there in case his arrival was seriously delayed. He knew I had only a one-way ticket, no way to get back, and very little money. And since this happened before cell phones were common, neither of us had one.

It was morning when my plane landed in Singapore. Terry was at my gate to meet me. I was so relieved and happy to see him. He was bursting all over with smiles. I remember thinking, I'm *going to like this guy.*

After leaving the airport, we took a taxi to the railroad station, and he bought two one-way tickets to Kuala Lumpur, Malaysia. Our journey was a long, slow ride covering 226 miles, allowing me to get to know him better. He held my hand for most of the trip and was polite and not forward in his manner.

At one point during the trip, he told me that there was an American Embassy in Kuala Lumpur where we could get my visa to enter the U.S.A. He made it sound easy, which, as it turned out, was not the case.

We finally got to Kuala Lumpur, and by late afternoon we took a taxi to the Hotel Mandarin, where we would stay for the night. It was a nice, clean place, and we were exhausted. I told Terry to take the first shower since he had traveled farther than me, 9,222 miles. After his shower, he came out wearing only his underwear.

It was my turn, and Terry was kind enough to help me adjust the shower controls to the correct temperature. I had never been inside a hotel room before, and when I showered at home, I was used to cold water only.

I stayed in the shower for a long time. Panic was beginning to set in. After all, this would be the first time I would be naked and alone with a man I hardly knew. I wrapped the towel around me, stepped from the shower and walked into the bedroom. I broke the ice, reached up, and pulled out my two front, false teeth. I smiled. Terry looked at me from the bed and smiled, too. Then we both laughed. I knew what was coming, or did I? Part of me was still scared.

I walked toward him, and stood in front of the bed upon which he was lying. He had become so aroused that he had difficulty removing his underwear. He pulled back the covers to let me lie next to him. As I let the towel drop to the floor, I said to myself, "*Well, here goes.*" He must have liked what he saw. I slid into the bed beside him and we slipped into each other with passion.

Terry then kissed my lips for the first time, which made me instantly wet and beyond ready. He turned and pulled out a condom from the nightstand drawer. When I saw this, I said, "No, condom, no condom." I wanted his baby. He could not resist me and tossed the condom to the floor, then slipped himself inside me. We climaxed together.

Afterward, we relaxed. A few minutes later, Terry turned to me and asked, "Was I big enough?" I thought, "He must be insecure, like me." And I said, "More than enough." He sighed, and a warm smile crossed his face.

The next morning, we walked to the government building that housed the American Embassy where we could apply for a marriage permit. We sat down at a wooden desk where sat, across from us, an official who seemed to be in charge. As the man looked up from what he was doing, Terry said, "Hello. We're here because we would like to obtain a license to get married."

The man said, "Can I please see your passports?" Terry handed our passports to the man. The man looked at them, then looked up at him and said, "Are you already married?" Terry said, "I was, but that was years ago." Then the man said, "Can I see your divorce papers?" Terry smiled and said, "Well, I don't usually carry them around with me."

The man frowned, and Terry asked him what he should do. It would be almost impossible to come up with a copy of that document. In answer, the man looked around the room, put his hand under the table, and tapped the underside several times. Terry reached for his wallet, and the man shook his head from side to side ever so slightly, whispering, "Not now."

In his normal voice, he said, "I will have to ask my boss for permission first, about the absent divorce papers." The man got up and went into another room, closing the door behind him. That was Terry's cue. I could see him reach for his wallet and, as inconspicuously as possible, pull out a one-hundred-ringgit note and put it in the palm of his right hand, then placing it in his lap under the table. When the man came back, he said, "Everything will be okay." He sat down and put his hand under the table, while Terry took the note from his lap and the man took it from him. Then the man typed up an official-looking document, which we both signed. He then notarized it many times, stamp, stamp, stamp. He was making it all official. He said we would next have to get it translated from Bahasa into English for the U.S. Embassy. He was accommodating and told us where to get that done.

However, getting it done took us another few days, and Terry told me that his money was running low. His American Express card was getting filled up. I was surprised when he told me this because I thought all Americans were wealthy.

The last thing we needed to do was find a witness who would stand up for us. And a judge who would preside over the celebration and be willing to marry us. The witness was easy to find. We asked the bellboy at our hotel, a charming Muslim fellow named Ariffin bin Bidin. Ariffin also knew where to get married. I wanted Terry to buy me a new wedding dress, but he told me he was near broke. He could see I was distraught, so we decided to settle on a beautiful new white skirt and blouse and new shoes. However, I could see that it hurt him that he could not afford to buy me a new wedding dress.

Because of the many stories I had heard, I believed that in America, money truly did grow on trees. The night before we got married, Terry became quite nervous and held me very close in bed. He then asked me if I thought, we were doing the right thing.

I said, "Of course we are." It seemed to me he was perhaps getting cold feet, so I made love to him, and when he woke up in the morning, his feet were warm.

Ariffin took us to the judge, a prominent Hindu Indian official, with a red dot on her forehead, called a bindi, which meant she was married. She took one look at Terry and said in good English, "If you are already married, you're going to be in big trouble!"

He said he was not. Then with Ariffin by our side, we recited our "I do's," and Terry placed a simple gold band on my ring finger. The date was August 18, 1993.

Another official typed up our marriage certificate in Bahasa and then gave us two copies, one on pink paper and the other on blue.

After the wedding, we went out to celebrate at an outdoor restaurant. We had been there more than a few times by then, because of the excellent food and friendly people. I ordered a Guinness Extra

Stout and got Terry a Tiger Beer. When the waiter served him, Terry was hesitant, as he put his hand around the cold bottle. It was then that I remembered he had told me he hadn't drunk any alcohol for years. I thought to myself, "but this is a special occasion." Then, he ordered the next one on his own.

The next day we went to the U. S. embassy to get my visa so Terry could take me home. No such luck. The clerk said since we were married, I could not get one. Terry would have to fly back to America, file papers from there, and wait three months. What he should have done was file for a fiancée visa, and I would have gotten one in a few days.

However, this idea sounded foolish because had Terry gone this route and brought me back to the United States with this fiancée visa. Without the commitment of having married me, he might have decided the whole thing was a bad idea. He could have quickly sent me back home, and that would have been that.

Yet, the only thing we could do now was to get a blood test for HIV and tuberculosis, which the American Embassy required. The clinic was a short walk away. I was seen by an Indian doctor, who made me disrobe without an assistant nearby.

He then felt my ample breasts for apparently no reason other than he had the opportunity to do so. I was there only for a blood test and an X-ray, and Terry could see this happening through a thin curtain between us but did not say anything. Afterward, he shook his head in disgust and told me the doctor was nothing more than a 'dirty old man.' There just didn't seem to be anything we could do about the doctor's harassment, especially since we didn't want to give him any reason to not fill out the paperwork. However, I passed all the tests, along with fulfilling this doctor's lewd and inappropriate needs.

Another stumbling block we encountered since Terry and I were already married was that I had to prove I wasn't married to my daughter's father. To do so, we had to fly back to Kuching, then drive twenty miles through the rain forest to my village of Kampung Gerung. Once there, we had to ask the village chief to sign an embassy document saying that I was not married to my daughter's father.

We went inside the chief's hut, then waited until the other elders showed up. After all, it wasn't an everyday thing for a white man, to suddenly show up in the village.

Within the hour, the eight other elders, all men, showed up, and we all sat on the floor in a circle. When Terry asked the chief to please sign the papers so he and I could get my visa, he looked at him and said in English, "You know, she is not a virgin. Why would you want to marry her?" Terry replied, "Because I love her." Then, the chief smiled and said, "You know, she has the biggest tits in our village." When I heard this, I smiled.

I had no idea that the chief was going to say those things, and when I looked at Terry to see how he would react, the look on his face told me that Terry didn't know what to say. He just kept his mouth shut and looked down at the floor. But I knew what to think, though I was not about to say it out loud: *I did have the biggest breasts in the village, and I was proud of them.*

Then came another test, which was something even I had not known about beforehand. One of the elders set down a clear glass gallon jug filled with small snakes, lizards that had just hatched, and chicken feathers. All of these contents were floating around into the jug, which was filled with rice wine.

The chief's wife came in and gave drinking glasses to everybody, except me. She poured some jungle wine from the jar into each glass. When all their glasses were filled, the elders became silent and stared at Terry. Even though I hadn't known what they were planning, I could see that they were waiting to see what he would do or say.

He held his glass up to his mouth and drank its contents down in one long, slow gulp. Within seconds, he began to sweat profusely. He looked at the others, who nodded with approval. Terry had passed the test. The others toasted him, then drank the contents of their glasses. The chief signed the embassy papers with his cryptic signature and then stamped each page accordingly with the village's official stamp. And, of course, as is the custom when dealing with any governmental agency where I come from, Terry then gave the chief a monetary donation.

The next day we flew back to Kuala Lumpur. When we got to the American Embassy, the guards checked us in, and then we went to the main lobby. Terry picked a number, and we waited patiently for our number to come up. Surprisingly, we got to see the same man as before.

When Terry pushed the papers that proved I wasn't married through the glass slot, the man didn't even bother to look at the documents. I was shocked, and thought to myself, *What an asshole.* Terry had spent a lot of extra time and money to get those papers, and this guy didn't even give us the common courtesy of looking at our paperwork. Stamp, stamp, stamp, and we had accomplished our task. Yet, we would have to wait another three months before we could once again be together.

All Terry could do was to take me to the airport for a flight back to Kuching. I felt sad because my heart was at long last beginning to open up to his love. We kissed and said a sad goodbye.

With a tear in my eye, I stopped before getting on the plane and looked back at him. He stood there, watching me board the plane to go home. As tears continued to well up in my eyes I could see that like me, there was a deep sadness in his eyes, too.

CHAPTER 6

A Change of Life

Three months was a long time to wait. I was so ready to start a new life in America with my new husband, and to give my daughter Aling opportunities that she would never have in Malaysia. But I had no choice but to wait. So, feeling sad and frustrated, I moved back in with my sister and went back to work at the salon. My co-workers were happy to see me, and I was glad to have them in my life, especially since I needed all the emotional support they could give me. Over the years, they had become my extended family.

When the Chinese man found out I was in Kuching, he started haunting me, for a part of me that I had promised to Terry. He would come to the salon to see me, but I would hide in the back, and my co-workers would cover for me.

One time he trapped me as I got off the bus near the salon. He started begging me to go out with him. It made me so angry when he did this, that I screamed, "Leave me alone! I'm married, and I don't want ever to see you again."

This one encounter embarrassed him because we were in front of many people. At first, he got outraged, and his eyes were ablaze. Then he caught himself and walked away. And that was the last of him for now, but I was still leery of what he might do in the future.

So, I waited. There was not much else I could do. Terry would call once a week and send money orders, which pleased me no end. Now, having more money than ever before, I was able to help my parents and my daughter.

When I told them about Terry, my father just nodded and smiled, saying very few words. That was just his way. My mother, though, did ask a few questions and was surprised that I had a relationship with a white guy from America. Neither of my parents nor Aling had ever met one before.

I hoped to be with my mother when she died. She would, however, pass away only a few days after I left for America, never having the chance to meet Terry. She was only sixty-five. I never found out what she died from, and even today, I still miss her very much.

In the weeks to follow, I would see very little of Aling. She was living in a government-sponsored boarding school near Kuching. The teachers at the village primary school helped her get accepted because of her stellar grades and positive attitude. Many children would quit after primary school and end up helping their parents, tending to the rice paddies, or not go to school at all.

By this time, my parents had moved from The Kampong. And they were living with my oldest sister and her husband, Embrose. Their home was just a few miles from Aling's boarding school. On some weekends, she would take a bus to visit them. At my sister's house I told Aling we would be leaving her for one year. If things were going well between Terry and me in America, I said, "We will come back and get you." My leaving didn't seem to bother her much. For most of her life, my parents had raised her, since she was a toddler. Yet, I wanted to make up for my absence from her life. Bringing her to America seemed like a good thing.

Soon after Terry got to the states, he called and said, "I've rented a nice apartment for us in Lincoln, Nebraska. It's only nine miles from my body shop in Eagle." He also said that he was overwhelmed by all the paperwork he had to fill out in order for us to be together again.

But what he was more concerned about was whether or not I was pregnant. One of the first things he would say was, "Have you had your period yet?" He asked this same question each time he called. Finally, toward the end of the month, it happened. I was not pregnant, much to his relief and my dismay. I very much wanted to have his baby!

Three months passed, and finally, my paperwork went through, and at last, Terry called to tell me he had received my visa in the mail. I was so happy that soon I would be with him again. He sent me tickets to Bangkok, where we would celebrate our honeymoon. He said, "Don't pack any clothes. I will buy you anything you need." I took him at his word, and when I got off the plane in Bangkok, all I carried was a small paper sack with one pair of pink silk panties. When I showed them to him, he smiled.

We touched hands to show our affection for one another. It was improper to offer any other gestures of love in public. Nevertheless, we both felt that spark of energy once again ignite our souls.

Terry already had a room for us since he had arrived the day before. He explained his early arrival to me, saying that he had wanted to make sure there would be no delays. And, of course, he added, he had wanted everything to be ready for my arrival. Our room was at The Grace Hotel, which was a thriving brothel, as we soon discovered. After all, this was Bangkok.

Our first night together in three months was pure passion! Next door, through the thin walls, we could hear the moans of another woman. Someone was making love to her with the rhythmic banging of the headboard against our adjoining wall. It was very erotic. After we climaxed, I lay back, wanting a cigarette but knew better. I thought to myself, *Terry and I are going to have a great sex life.*

Later that evening, we went down to eat in the hotel's restaurant. As we sat quietly, I brushed my hand gently against his Terry's white skin, which Terry responded to by looking at me and smiling.

Then he said, "What are you doing?" to which I answered, "I wish I could have your white skin." He reacted in a way I thought was strange, and seemed to be taken aback, saying, "What's so special about white?"

I thought for a few seconds. When I replied, "I think white people have more money," Terry was silent.

After dinner we walked together through the streets of Bangkok. There were a number of beggars, many of them children with severed arms or legs. Later, we discovered that some parents would disfigure their babies at birth. To them, begging was just a job. And having a disabled child, they figured, would be to their advantage.

Farther down the street, a vendor who spoke English stopped us and said, "I've heard the word 'sugar daddy' many times," when he was selling his wares to a white guy and his young Asian girlfriend. He asked, "What does 'sugar daddy' mean?" I sheepishly smiled and pointed at Terry, who then went on to explain to him what the term meant.

Wanting to explore Bangkok, I decided I would follow Terry's lead. He seemed to know what he was doing, and anyway, I didn't have much choice. I had never been anywhere before I met Terry, nor did I have the money to do so. After all, he was my 'Sugar Daddy.' And I felt safe with him.

Terry then asked a Tuk Tuk driver where we could go at night to have a fun time. The driver was thin and wore a soiled T-shirt and shorts. His bare feet were heavily calloused. He smiled and said, "We go to Phat Pong." We climbed into his three-wheeled open scooter, and we were on our way.

For a good half hour, we sped, weaving through the crowded and heavily polluted streets. I held onto Terry tightly as we quickly careened from one side of the road to the other. By the time the driver stopped at the entrance to a long, multi-colored neon-lit street, darkness had already fallen. There were no cars in sight, just a mass of people with the blasting sound of music drifting over the crowd toward us.

The driver, with a sweep of his arm, said, "We have arrived. Phat Pong!" At the end of his gesture, his open palm stopped in front of Terry's face, which I realized was his unsubtle way of saying, "Pay me now." He paid the driver, including a small tip.

After walking for a while, we sat down on an old loading dock and watched the parade of people pass by. They all seemed to be very busy, looking from one side of the street to the other with purpose and direction.

After a few minutes, a young girl approached us and asked, in English, "May I please sit beside you?" We both nodded yes, and the girl took a seat and moved very close to Terry. At first, I felt sorry for her. She had pulled tight the belt around her small waist, a distraction that didn't fit her youthful good looks. When she smiled, I could see that one of her front teeth was missing.

She started asking us questions about one thing and another, and after a few minutes, Terry began to nudge me to move over. I thought nothing of it at the time, but finally, he jumped down from the dock and said, "Okay, Pedo. It's time for us to go." The girl took off fast. Terry looked at me and said, "That girl was trying to pick my pocket!" Which pissed me off. Because nobody was going to have their hand in my man's pocket but me. Was this a preview of what we would be up against down the street?

As we walked through the tunnel of colored neon lights, the crossfire of booming music from both sides caught us off guard. Bar after bar lined the street, some with kickboxing rings, others swarming with men and hovering hookers. I saw Terry take his wallet from his rear pocket and put it in his right front for safer keeping.

Then a skinny Thai guy jumped in front of us, shouting above the noise and music, "Live sex show, cheap beer, no cover charge!" We looked at each other in tacit agreement and followed him up two flights of old wooden stairs to a heavily used door. As he opened it for us, the smell of stale beer, thick cigarette smoke, and loud music poured over us like a gathering storm. The room was populated mostly by men. We sat towards the back, facing a small wooden stage. Within seconds a very sexy young hooker sat down beside Terry and asked us if we wanted a threesome interplay. She must have thought that I, too, was a hooker. I didn't blame her for the mistake; I was wearing a sexy outfit and looked as hot as her, if not more so. We told her, "Thank you for the offer, but no thanks." But she continued to talk with Terry so she could practice her English. The barmaid came up to the table and took our order. When the drinks came, Terry paid, smiled, and gave her a generous tip.

Then the house lights dimmed, the stage lights came on, and the hooker beside Terry disappeared into the dark. Soft music came on, and most of the crowd fell silent. From stage left, a naked young girl who looked about seventeen appeared. She was short and fairly nice looking, but a tad overweight. A few men in the audience began to boo, but she walked on undaunted, and looking very bored, soon left the stage. Next came a naked, tall, and beautiful Thai woman with a great body. I felt a tinge of jealousy as Terry sat up straight in his chair and took close notice as she crossed the stage. She stopped at center stage, and I saw a white string hanging down between her long legs. I thought perhaps this woman had her period and had forgotten to take out her tampon. Her eyes panned the audience of men and held fast upon one man in particular, and I was upset that it seemed she was looking directly at my man. Slowly, she opened her legs wide, then gently pulled the string from inside her. I was shocked to see, one after the other, six double-edged razor blades emerge, each attached to the string. My first thought was that this woman must risk serious pain to herself, and that thought made me feel pain as I couldn't help imagining how it must feel. Then I felt a sense of shame come over me, feeling shame for this woman who apparently made a living doing such a dangerous, painful act. And yet, at the same time, I was also intrigued to see what she would do next.

Her next gynecological feat involved putting ping pong balls into her vagina, then bending over and shooting them at the audience's cheering men. The men who sat in the front row caught most of the balls. Appearing to need a relaxing break, she took out a cigarette, lit it, but instead of putting it into her mouth, she placed the filtered end of the cigarette into her vagina. She then somehow seemed to inhale the lit cigarette with her vagina, then remove it as if she was taking it from her mouth, and then, bizarrely exhaling the smoke from her vagina onto the audience. And there I sat, craving a cigarette but not daring to smoke in front of Terry.

Finally, she took a full 12-ounce bottle of Coke, which she opened, then threw the cap into the audience. Then she lay down on her back, kicked her legs up into the air, and sucked the bottle's entire contents into her vagina. She stood up, strutted around the stage three times, then squatted down over the empty bottle and refilled it to the top. She picked up the Coke and offered it to a guy who was sitting in the front row, who took it. And with that, the tall, beautiful Thai woman blew a kiss to the audience and sauntered off stage.

For the grand finale, a tall, lean Thai man sporting a huge erection came out on stage, followed by another beautiful young girl.

She bent over, grabbed her ankles, and then proceeded with pleasure to take a pounding from the remarkably well endowed man for quite a while. She then smiled and left the stage, followed by the man who, incredibly, still seemed to be as hard as a rock.

As the show came to an end, we got up to leave, but a huge muscular Thai man stopped us at the door, demanding money. Terry told him he paid for the beer. The overpowering man looked him in the face and said, "You have to pay to leave." Terry turned and looked at me. And then, without argument, he paid the muscular man.

We then walked to the quiet end of Phat Pong, and there we came upon a statue of a Golden Buddha, his hands cupped before him as if he were asking for an offering. We both knelt before the Buddha and said a silent prayer. I prayed for a good life; what Terry prayed for, I will never know. We flagged down another Tuk, Tuk motor scooter, and went back to the hotel. As we made love that night, it was hard for me to forget what we had seen in Phat Pong, and I will always remember that strange sex show. The next day we boarded our flight to America, which would be a new adventure and a profound change of life for me.

CHAPTER 7

Walking into a freezer.

As I stepped aboard the enormous plane, I couldn't imagine how much of a change I would be going through once we arrived in Terry's home country. My emotions were flipping back and forth, from fear to joy, wondering what lay ahead in my future. The plane was packed tight with people in what they called "economy class."

At Terry's request we sat in the non-smoking section, it made little difference, since there were no walls between us and the smoking section, so the smoke circulated throughout the plane.

I became nervous and envied the smokers. If only I could have just one to calm me! I thought of smoking in the toilet, but the sign said it would make an alarm go off. So, I toughed it out.

With a thud, skip, and a roar, the plane landed, then on the ground kept rolling--Terry said it was "taxiing"-- towards the terminal. A stewardess came on over the intercom, telling us first in English and then in Chinese, "Please remain in your seats with your seatbelts buckled until the plane comes to a complete stop." Many passengers ignored the request, as I heard the unclicking of seatbelts all around me. Within seconds passengers stood in the aisles, maneuvering one way or another as they struggled to retrieve their luggage from the overhead bins. Terry and I stayed in our seats until the bustle settled down.

When we entered the terminal, first we had to go through immigration. Above us, there was a large sign in blue and white, which said, "Welcome to the United States of America." When I saw that sign, tears formed in my eyes. Behind us, there were hundreds of people of various nationalities in a tightly packed switchback of lines. It was over an hour before we finally got to one of the immigration officers, who was young and kind. He looked at all of my paperwork, and then, with a smile and a nod, went stamp, stamp, stamp. As he handed back my papers, he said, "Welcome to America, Miss." I was now officially in the United States. Next came customs, which was similarly uneventful because we had nothing to declare and very little luggage. At least this first time.

We had to sprint to catch our first connecting flight, to Minneapolis/ St. Paul, and we got to the gate just in time. It was a much shorter flight, only three hours, and we arrived very early in the morning. There we had to wait for the last flight of our journey to Lincoln, Nebraska.

By then I was dog-tired, and snuck off to one of the airport bathrooms. Once in the bathroom, I took out my one pack of cigarettes. I simply had to have a cigarette! When I lit one up and sucked the smoke down into my lungs I forgot about my past and, at that moment, felt perfectly serene. I exhaled, and as the smoke left my mouth, I realized I was in a bathroom in a foreign country.

The last flight was in a much smaller plane, which Terry called a turboprop. It was different in many ways from the previous big jet planes. For starters, it had propellers instead of jet engines. And it was so cramped that Terry had to stoop over as we walked down the narrow aisle with only one seat on either side. Also, it didn't have a bathroom, and I wondered how the pilots would relieve themselves if they needed to. Also, why there weren't any stewardesses? I didn't know then that those small turboprops never flew long distances.

The plane roared off to a bumpy, heart-stopping flight. Lucky for me, it was short. Before I knew it, it landed the way it took off, with a thud, skip and bounce before taxiing over to the airport. I was glad this flight was over.

It was night when the airplane door opened to the tarmac, and the second the outside air hit me, I had to brace myself. I felt like I was walking into a freezer. It was November, and the temperature was seventeen degrees. Back in Borneo, the average year-round temperature was eighty. It was just a short walk from the airplane to the warmth of the terminal, and once in there, Terry told me he had left his car in the parking lot, which was just another short walk. But it wasn't nearly so short.

He held my hand as we crossed the icy pavement, a new experience for my feet. And dressed in a light sweater and red high heels, I was freezing. He hadn't warned me about how cold it would be when we arrived, and I wished I had thought to ask him about the weather. I didn't have any real cold-weather clothing, but if I'd known it was going to be so very cold, I could at least have brought more layers of clothing to wear for the walk to his car.

At last, Terry pointed toward his car, which sat isolated under a lamppost, as snow--another new experience for me-- sprinkled across the windshield. It was a white rusted-out 1978 Datsun B210 that looked like a refugee from a junkyard. My heart sank. I was expecting a newer car, not this old piece of junk. He then stuck his finger into a hole in the driver's door to click it open and then reached down for a screwdriver from under the seat to open the trunk. He then loaded our bags. With the same screwdriver, which he stuck into the ignition, the car came to life, and within a few minutes, blessedly warm air began to fill the car.

I began to warm up, but my mind was reeling as we drove into the night. If my wealthy American's car was like this, in what condition would I find my new home? I was beginning to panic.

We arrived at Terry's apartment complex; ours was on the ground floor. As he reached into his pocket for the key, I hoped he would not pull out another screwdriver.

He didn't carry me over the threshold as I had seen in some movies, but that was okay by me. And the apartment, thankfully, was nice, clean, and warm. I was desperate for a cigarette, but I didn't want to stink up our home. So I wrapped myself in a blanket and went outside to smoke. As I stood there in the cold, inhaling on my cigarette, I thought to myself, "Stupid. What are you doing out here?" I had a choice between a loving man and a warm water bed, or a cigarette. I dropped the cigarette and ground it out under my shoe, and decided then and there that I had smoked my last smoke.

The next day Terry took me to meet his children and grandchildren, who all lived in Lincoln. They were very accepting of me and I of them. I even met his ex-wife, and we got along well for months, until I started to feel jealous of her.

We then drove the ninety miles to St. Paul, Nebraska, to meet his mother, Marie, who was widowed. Terry's mother made quite an impression on me, and as time passed, she would be like another mom to me. One thing we both had in common was our height and weight. She stood 4 feet, eleven inches tall. Five inches taller than me, and she weighed just under one hundred pounds, as did I. We would remain close to those numbers for the rest of her life.

Terry had to go back to work in his body shop, and I followed him as if we were cemented together, like Siamese twins. When we got there, I saw the building was an old two-bay gas station right off the highway in Eagle.

When he opened the door, he told me to close my eyes as he held my hand and led me inside. Once inside, we stopped, and he said, "Open your eyes." In front of me was a hot pink 1974 Volkswagen Beetle, a wedding gift that he had gotten for his new bride. He had restored it while he was waiting for my visa to arrive.

But his heart sank when I told him I couldn't drive a stick shift. In addition to that, I didn't even have a driver's license. So, Terry sold my Volkswagen Beetle and bought me a black Ford with an automatic transmission, and painted a pink stripe on it. And with my persistent requests, he finally gave up his white Datsun B210 to the local junkyard.

My only problem now was figuring out how I would get my driver's license? My writing and reading skills in English happened to be less than proficient. If the tests had been in Chinese, Bhasa, or Malay, I would have had a better chance. Anyway, it took me three times, but I finally passed both the written and the road test. I would not give up.

For the first few weeks, I would sit in the body shop office with my feet in front of an electric heater. It was still very cold to me. Of course, Terry told me all I had to do was nothing but to sit there and look pretty. He said he would take care of me, which he did. My man was a hard worker.

But when spring came, I was tired of just sitting. I watched Terry work hard day after day, and then before long, I started to see many things that I could do to help. So, bit by bit, he showed me how to do various tasks, and as with my uncle, I was a fast learner. Over time, I came to work with my husband full time. We had a good relationship at home and in bed, and now, also at work.

Soon after the hot pink bug sold, it got around town that our body shop was the place to go to get vehicles restored. Then a Lincoln newspaper came out to the shop and took pictures of another Volkswagen bug we were working on together. They called it a human interest story. After that, we had more work than we could do at times. In the end, we came to restore over one hundred Volkswagen Beetles. I did the refurbishing work on the interiors and Terry handled the bodywork and paint on the outside.

We even ended up doing one that a couple brought to us from Colorado on a trailer. The husband and wife came into the office, and Terry and I went outside to look at it. It was a robin's-egg blue 1969 convertible 'bug,' but it was in the same condition as his old white Datsun he had taken to the junkyard. Maybe even a tad worse. We then went back into the office and told them they could buy a brand new 'bug' for what it would cost to restore this one.

The man's wife looked at us and said, "I don't care what it will cost. I want it done!" Her husband remained silent for a few seconds. Then, with a sigh, he said, "Okay. Let's unload it."

Terry and I worked on that bug for months. Thirty thousand dollars of work and materials later, we had completed the job, which looked to be in show-room shape, which happened to be perfect timing, since we needed the money to fly back to Borneo and pick up my daughter, Aling.

Then, one day, Dick Carr, the man who owned a farm across the way, came over to talk with Terry and me. He said, "I've been watching you two for a few months now, and I like the way you work. My son and I want to start a car lot and call it Carr's Cars. I have an empty building, larger than the one you've got here, and if you want, I'd like you to use it as your new body shop. You wouldn't have to worry about rent; work it off as I need bodywork on our vehicles. It would be a good deal for all of us. What do you say?"

Terry and I walked across the street to look at the building. It was big and empty and full of potential. Dick even said he would furnish a huge wood-burning stove, along with a bathroom. We would build a paint booth and turn the hayloft into a bedroom, though that, unfortunately, turned out to be problematic for us.

Before long, the new shop was working well, and in time Dick became our surrogate father. He was certainly old enough. Also, Dick taught us a crucial lesson on how to handle our money. He could pinch a nickel into a dime. And his son Joe became like a brother to Terry. They would often joke around with others, saying, "Yeah, we're brothers with different mothers."

We moved from our apartment in Lincoln to our new home, saving money and time on driving back and forth. But what turned out very nice was our loft, the 'love-nest' of our lives. Terry bought a new TV and a queen-sized bed, and the sex was great! And on top of that, we could pick our own' work hours.

At night, as we slept, our hormones would whisper to one another. Many times, I would wake him up to make love again. One time I woke him up at 3:00 AM, and he said, "Go to sleep, Pedo, I'm tired." I never forgot that he said, 'no," to me when I was more than ready for him to take me. But payback is hell, and I sadly took out my revenge on more than one occasion.

Over time, my periods became more and more painful. I would tell Terry to do something for me. I'm sure he felt helpless as he pushed on my tummy, as I had told him to do. I wanted his baby in the worst way, but I had already had three miscarriages by this time. Each time I would blame him, saying, "Your seed just don't stick." It tore up my heart and made me very sad, every time I had my period. I really wanted to have a baby with Terry.

Then my bleeding worsened, so Terry took me to a female gynecologist who was also a surgeon and a lovely person. She told us that if I did not have a hysterectomy, I would end up in the ER, bleeding to death from fibrous tumors. I think that that scared him more than it did me.

I had the surgery, as she removed my uterus, ovaries, and fallopian tubes. The good doctor told me that she had not removed my cervix because she felt I would still want to have feeling in my vaginal canal. We were happy about that. The doctor saved all the parts and showed them to Terry because he always wanted to learn about things. Later, he told me that my uterus looked like a big angry fist.

After I came out from recovery, the doctor told us that everything went well, but she warned us, "I don't want you to have sex for two weeks." Terry stayed with me that night in the hospital, then took me home the next morning.

But that next night, every remaining hormone in my body had settled in my vagina. And we came together like a magnet to steel. I was puffy, tight, and wet as he entered me. It was great sex, even though I bled some, though not too much. To be safe, however, we went back to the doctor the following day. She looked at my vagina with a cold steel speculum.

Terry asked if he could take a look, too. The doctor said, "Sure," so he took a look at my cervix close up. And he said it looked like a small round pink donut with a tiny hole in the center. I smiled and told him, "Now you know what the end of your penis is rubbing up against when we make love."

The doctor found nothing wrong with me and, as she picked up my small silk panties, said, "These sure are cute." Terry smiled and said, "Just like my wife." The doctor, too, smiled and said to us, "Try and be good, all right?" We tried that night but once again had a difficult time resisting each other.

CHAPTER 8

Aling Coming to America.

Above is a picture of Aling and Pedo rollerblading while living in Kuala Lumpur.

It was time to fly back to Kuching and bring back my daughter; a year had passed quickly. However, living in the shop with Aling would not work out, so we rented a two-bedroom apartment near the one we were in before moving above the shop. It was nice, clean, and located on the third floor, which also had a nice balcony, an added feature which I liked very much.

The next morning Terry drove my Ford to the Lincoln airport and left it in long-term parking. It was the first of January and very cold; I felt sorry for my car, as well as myself. The flights back to Kuching were, as before, long and boring. But I was excited about bringing my daughter back to America. And so was Terry. I knew in my heart that Aling would excel here, in the land of opportunity. Also, I was excited to tell my friends about America, even though it had been quite a change for me.

When the plane landed in Kuching, the flight attendant opened the cabin door. The familiar blast of rain forest mist quickly consumed our breathing. Terry gasped, but I inhaled deeply, filling my lungs with the moist air and enjoying the first moment of being home once again. Terry, though, wiped away the beads of sweat from his forehead with the back of his hand. It was an abrupt night to day shift for him, from the everchanging, and at that time of year, much colder weather of Nebraska.

We took a taxi to Embrose and Jaming's house, which held some haunting memories of being returned back to my uncle many times. They must have heard our taxi pull up in front of their home because shortly afterward, Embrose and my sister, Jaming, came out of the house to greet us with open arms and big smiles. Terry got along well with Embrose, who spoke English excellently, compared to my sister Jaming, who spoke it not at all. Terry's Bahasa skill was comparable to Jaming's English, since all he knew was the word for 'hello.' So, they mostly smiled and nodded at each other. I was somewhat embarrassed when he asked me why my sister's lips were stained red. I explained that she chewed betel nuts, a form of Malaysian tobacco that grows wild on palm trees. I'm sure he was happy the red of my lips came from lipstick and not from Bidayuh lipstick, as they called it.

That night we slept in an upstairs room, a far cry from our apartment home in Lincoln. It was hot, humid, noisy, and full of mosquitos. Terry, however, seemed to adapt to it quickly. He had to; after all, I was his wife.

The next morning, Terry woke up to the roosters' annoying crowing in the backyard, which moved him to wake me up. I was irritated, being in the midst of deep sleep after our long travels from the day before. But I bit my tongue before I could say anything coarse to him, realizing we had never been bothered by rooster crows back in Lincoln, Nebraska. Anyway, the day before we had planned to meet up today with Aling in a cafe close to her boarding school. Jaming's son, who lived nearby, agreed to make sure Aling would be there on time to meet her new dad.

The bus would arrive in the early afternoon, stopping in front of the house for the ten-mile ride. Embrose, Jaming, Terry, and I walked across a small footbridge that crossed a creek to get to the road where the bus would stop. Sadly, that bridge would play a significant role in my husband's life in the future. The bus soon arrived, and as we stepped into the old bus, I had a flash of memory of when my uncle had dragged me onto it screaming several years earlier. But that thought vanished as I sat down, thinking I would never have to ride it again. Within a few days, this experience would be thousands of miles away in my mind and body with my husband and daughter back in America.

We arrived at the cafe and sat down at a large round table where seven of my relatives waited for us. This meeting, of course, was a big event for them. I could only hope they and my daughter, Aling, would like Terry as much as I did. Everybody ordered food and drinks, but I was a little worried since Aling's chair was still empty. I was beginning to think that perhaps she had had second thoughts and had been scared away . After all, this was going to be a life-changing time for her.

I was still thinking about this when, out of nowhere, my twelve-year-old daughter appeared, skinny, somewhat nervous, and, as I had expected, a tad shy. I looked at her and smiled, nudging Terry to let him know it was her, because he had never seen even a picture of her. Terry stood up and held his hand out to her; she shook it and gave him a guarded smile. Without saying a word, she then started walking around the table, sneaking glances at Terry but not taking her seat to join us for food.

Her silent treatment hurt me deeply because it had been one year since I saw her last, and I missed her. But then I realized that I couldn't really blame her if she didn't feel immediately drawn to me. After all, when she was little, I was poor and on my own, so my parents had raised her for most of her life, and we hadn't had much of a chance to get to know each other. I had just provided money for her room and board. Ours was nothing like any kind of normal mother/daughter relationship, and in that sense, though she was, like me, separated from her mother when she was young, it also meant that at the moment, we were little more than strangers.

We all spoke our jungle language during the meal, leaving Terry out, for the most part. He knew only a few words, important ones like "hello, bathroom, goodbye, I love you, and "Please give me one more beer." As time went on, I taught him more words, but it seemed to me Terry was somewhat 'hard in his head' when it came to acquiring a new language.

When the meal was over and we said our goodbyes, I suddenly felt a moment of panic. I realized for the first time that I didn't know if I would ever see my family again. I was a little dazed by that. But when Terry, Aling, and I took a taxi back to Embrose's house Aling spoke a little to me, though not to Terry. Her shyness didn't really surprise me, though. I thought she must surely feel some uncertainty and was probably more than a bit terrified about the trip into the unknown she was going to take with us in a few days.

When we arrived at Embrose's house and I walked through the door, I found a surprise waiting for me. My dad was there. Ever since my mother had died, he would pass himself around to his many children's homes, staying for a few weeks at one place, 'til he tired of it, then moving on to the next.

I said hello to him, but was surprised when Aling ran up to him and gave him a big hug.

At first, it angered me because he had never hugged me, nor had he ever shown me any warmth or emotional support. But, I suppose, I was happy for Aling, knowing that she had lived with the family and felt like part of it, as I had never felt.

The neighbors who lived behind Embrose's house had acquired a rotary phone, and they were kind enough to call us a taxi to pick us up in the morning so Terry could adopt Aling and get her a visa to travel with us back to America. Afterward, we went upstairs to our bedroom and found another surprise. Embrose had put up mosquito netting around our bed, which made us both very happy. Aling slept beside her grandfather, as I had done with mine when I was young.

The next morning, , the roosters told us when it was time to get up. The taxi soon came to take us to the government adoption agency in Kuching. Embrose came along for emotional support, and because he spoke English and Bahasa. Terry's adoption of Aling was a big deal since neither she nor I had seen her father for over twelve years. He was simply out of both of our lives, yet someone needed to be there to sign the adoption papers on his behalf, to set her free. Embrose was the likely choice.

Fortunately, the man behind the desk was helpful as well as understanding. I explained Aling's biological father's problem in my language, while Terry had to sit and listen, not knowing or understanding what we said. The man then wrote out my story in longhand in Bahasa and then signed it. Then he turned to Aling and said, nodding toward Terry, "Do you want to be adopted by this man, and go to America?"

She looked at me, then at Terry, and said, "Yes." I then signed the paper, then Terry did, and finally, Embrose signed for the absent sperm donor, Hee Ping. Stamp, stamp, stamp. And, in this way, I finally gave my husband his beautiful new daughter.

After the official adoption, we all went back to Embrose and Jaming's house, where Jaming cooked us a big meal to celebrate while wondering aloud if she would ever see us again. I slept well that night beside Terry. He was not only a good man; he was my man.

The next morning, we took the same taxi, after the rooster's crow, and said our goodbyes. It all happened very fast, with no time for tears. The next stop was the Kuching airport, for a flight to Kuala Lumper to get Aling's visa for entry to the United States.

It was a short bumpy flight of one hour and forty-five minutes in a small jetliner. And we all sat together, like any family. Aling appeared stoic as she sat in the window seat, watching as the plane rose into the air and flew away from her homeland. Remembering how I felt when I flew away from Kuching for the first time, I couldn't help wondering whether she, too, must now be wondering whether she would ever return to see her home, her jungle family, and her friends again. It was a huge change of life for her. A bit over an hour later, the plane landed in the pouring rain with a thud and a roar. As it taxied toward the terminal, I saw my daughter still gripping tight the armrests on both sides of her. This trip was her first flight ever in an airplane.

With what little luggage we had, we took a taxi to a Holiday Inn close to the American Embassy. There, later that night in our room, Aling lay down in the first real bed she had ever slept in. I could tell she liked it.

That night, I was very nervous about what my daughter would have to go through on the morrow: the same embarrassing doctor's physical, like the one I had to get for my visa. And then all the paperwork that someone needed to fill out to complete the process. But that would be Terry's problem, not mine.

The room was on the tenth floor. Terry and Aling went outside on the small balcony, which gave a full view of the Petronas Twin Towers, among the world's tallest buildings. It was a spectacular sight, especially at night, all lit up. I was sure she was quite impressed, having never seen anything above one or two stories before as I.

As I sat on the edge of our bed watching them interact, I could tell my daughter was struggling with rudimentary English, as Terry would patiently listen, smile and nod. At that moment, my heart soared, knowing that I had made the right choice of a man not only for myself but also for Aling.

It was late in the day, and I was hungry. While sitting on the edge of our bed, I waved them in from the balcony. I said, "It's time to eat." Terry spoke up and said, "Let's get a pizza." Part of him suspected that Aling might have never eaten pizza before. I said, "I want chicken and rice." Then, Terry got a tad persistent as he looked at me. I could tell he really wanted the pizza.

At that moment, I flashed back in time to my grandfather in the jungle village where the women were subservient to the men when we brought them the snake meat. I also thought of my uncle's cruelty toward me, and then of Hee Ping, the man who tore my heart open with his abandonment.

All I could think was, *No man is ever going to control me or inflame my emotions again.* As Terry turned to leave the room, I stood up on the bed and jumped onto his back, and screamed into his ear, "I want chicken and rice!"

He pulled me off his back, and tossed me onto the bed, looking both confused and shocked. Aling just stared at us, looking confused and more than a little frightened.

I had no good words to explain what I had done, so I abruptly left the room, took the elevator down to the lobby, went outside, and stood there, letting the warm rain pour over me as I pouted. I got soaked, but I didn't care, and the wetness on my skin helped me calm down. Soon they both came down looking for me, and we quietly walked over to a cafe where Aling and I had chicken and rice while Terry ate eggs and rice.

I was not sorry about my sudden outburst, nor did I apologize to Terry. I still thought I needed to draw a line in the sand when it came to him and me. No man would ever take advantage of me again, not even Terry. I did wonder, though, whether perhaps the line I had drawn was too deep.

The next morning, we were off to the American Embassy to pick up Aling's visa. I was still apprehensive about the physical and the paperwork. But my fears would soon disappear. The doctor who took care of her was a kind and modest man, nothing like the one who had examined me. We then slid all the paperwork through the slot in the window at the embassy and stamp, stamp, stamp. The man behind the window handed Aling her visa for the U.S.A., her new home. We had done it. Aling was coming to America.

CHAPTER 9

THE JOURNEY BACK TO THE STATES

After we got Aling's visa, the stress was off me. We went back to the hotel to prepare and pack for the long grueling flight back to America.

We were hungry and found a cafe nearby that served both Asian and western food. Terry finally got his pizza, and Aling and I had Lahsa. We all ate to our hearts' desire. Having Lahsa was a real treat for me, because it was hard for me to adjust to western food, and I never would do so completely.

That night after our daughter went to sleep, Terry and I snuggled like spoons in bed. I felt somewhat guilty about having jumped on my husband's back before dinner the night before. So, I let him slide into me as nature would have it.

The next morning we took the hotel shuttle to the KL international airport, a very long ride. Terry and I held hands and spoke little because we were both nervous about the long, cramped, and dull flight ahead of us in economy class.

Aling talked a little in English with her new dad during the ride. She was a fast learner, and I thought it was lucky that she had some introductory English classes at the boarding school. When the shuttle bus arrived at the airport, the driver pulled our carry-on luggage from the rear of the small bus. As I watched Terry tip him, I had to grit my teeth as I thought back to when he decided not to tip me at the salon when we first met. His soon-to-be wife, an Asian beauty, was overlooked, while this old man got a tip without a second thought. I then relaxed, put this bad memory at the back of my mind, where sadly, it was always too easy to retrieve.

The KL airport is a huge, beautiful, and well-designed building with thousands of travelers running about, people of many different nationalities, languages, and types of dress. This bustling sight surprised Aling as we went inside, as it did me a year earlier.

I saw her reach for her dad's hand, even though he was carrying all of our baggage, except for my handbag. The sight of her instinctive movement was a little sad for me to see. I realized that she knew he would keep her safe and provide comfort, because he was a big, strong white American, an experienced traveler, and most importantly, a man. I wished she would have taken my hand instead. After all, she was my daughter. As Terry adjusted the luggage and took her hand, I realized she was beginning to bond with her new father. I let go of my jealous feelings and remembered how my husband had connected with me the first time he saw me, as Aling was now doing with him.

As we boarded the massive plane, we lucked out when the stewardess motioned for us to take the bulkhead seats with lots of leg-room. As we fastened our seatbelts, along with everyone else, the plane started to taxi down the tarmac to the runway for takeoff.

It seemed like it was taking forever, but the pilot then came on over the intercom in an attempt to make light of the situation when he said, "This is your Captain speaking. The co-pilot and I decided to drive the plane to our first layover in Japan instead of flying." Most of the passengers, including Terry, laughed at his joke. But Aling and I didn't understand. It would take us years to catch on to the American sense of humor, and even then, we were often puzzled over some joke, trying to figure out what was said in jest, and what wasn't. Neither of us had grown up with much western culture, televisions or films, so cultural references hat were obvious to people who, like Terry, grew up in the U.S. or another western society, were often foreign to us.

After a few more minutes, the plane slowed even more, turned, and stopped. It was time for takeoff. Then with a thundering roar, it we started moving again, and the plane went down the runway faster and faster, while the overhead luggage compartments shook and rattled. Aling and I held on tight to our seat armrests, but I could see that Terry was smiling, and leaning back into his seat to feel the full thrust of the engines. Then, poof. Suddenly, the plane was off the ground, the noise was much quieter, and as we rose higher and higher, the sky was a beautiful blue. And yes. We were bound for America.

After the smooth and powerful takeoff that was just heavenly, it turned into hell over the Pacific. It seemed as if demons had their claws on the plane, shaking it to pieces. Passengers' drinks were hurled to the ceiling, and food fell to the floor.

I could see panic in the eyes of people around us, and some of the other passengers started to pray. One man tried to leave the restroom, and the sound of the open door banging back and forth behind him startled me. The pilot told everyone to stay in their seats and buckle up; there was little humor in his voice this time around. The flight attendants struggled to reach their jump seats and fasten their seatbelts. Even they looked scared, which only made it worse for me because I was already petrified. I held Aling's hand tightly to comfort her, but she suddenly pulled it from my grip, then unbuckled her seatbelt and threw herself face down to the floor. Later, when the plane was no longer shaking like it was going to fall apart, she told me she'd felt as though she was about to throw up.

The turbulence lasted for ten minutes maybe even longer, until finally the plane found some smooth sailing, but until that happened, the turbulence felt like it would last for hours. The cabin lights came on steady, and there was a sigh of relief throughout the aircraft. Aling sat back down, still suffering from motion sickness. The plane was back to normal, but not our daughter. When the stewardesses served the food trays, as soon as she smelled the food she darted to the bathroom.

We landed at the Tokyo International Airport in Japan, several hours later with no ill effects from the flight except being tired of sitting. And Terry had a sore butt because he never had much of one in the first place. The layover was most welcome to all three of us.

The flight to from Tokyo to Los Angeles was longer than the flight from Kuala Lumpur and tedious, but I was grateful. I had had enough of flight turbulence to last me a lifetime. The smooth flight gave me time to think about how I would deal with my daughter full time, which would be new for both of us. Would I be a good mother and role model?

The plane landed with a skip, a skid, and a bounce. The customs line was long, longer than the line I'd waited in before. There were hundreds of people, and I had to pee but held it in. When we got to the immigration officer, I was scared, as I was before, so I let Terry do the talking. He then handed the man our passports and Aling's paperwork. The officer looked up and smiled at her, and said, "Welcome to America." Then, stamp, stamp, stamp. We were home.

The first thing I did after leaving immigration was to find a restroom. At least I didn't need a cigarette like last time. But the thought crossed my mind.

That night we stayed at a Hilton near the airport, taking a shuttle from the terminal, and of course, Terry tipped the driver. I bit my tongue. It was going to take me longer to get over my resentment about not tipping me when we first met. When we entered our room, Aling was taken aback by the luxury compared to her boarding school. We all took showers to wash off the long travel.

That's when it all started, Aling's first long-term love affair. She turned on the TV, and the first thing that came on was the "I Love Lucy" show; that affair--her love of television--would be everlasting, unlike future youthful love affairs that didn't last but did blossom and bear fruit.

The next flight was to Minneapolis, a shorter, welcome, uneventful, and smooth ride. And another layover. By now, we were all tired of flying, but we still had one more flight before we would be back in Nebraska. The last flight to Lincoln was, like last time, in a tiny turboprop airplane, the same one I flew in a year ago. But time did not soften the short flight. I still felt as though I was riding on an unbridled, saddle-less bucking water buffalo on steroids.

But by this time, I was getting used to rough flights, but Aling was not. She was glued to her seat, hands tight on the armrests, and her eyes were squeezed into thin lines. On the other hand, Terry sat way in the back of the small craft where it was the worst ride. He enjoyed the buffalo. Then the ride smoothed out, and it turned eerily quiet as the small craft slowly descended through the clouds. I looked out the window and saw a blanket of snow covering the landscape, the city lights of Lincoln twinkling like stars in the night.

The landing was smooth like butter as if preparing us for the opening of the cabin door. It was a slap in the face of freezing sleet well below zero. Aling was stunned; it took her breath away.

I finally had my family together. My daughter was thirteen now, my husband forty-six, and myself thirty-six. The year was 1995. As we walked towards the parking lot to get my Ford, I was worried about having my daughter with us because up till now I had always had my husband to myself, along with all of his attention. Now, I would have to share that attention.

But that thought vanished when I saw my Ford! The cold and drizzling weather had encased it in a thin sheet of ice. Terry had the key to unlock the door, but the lock was frozen solid. He said if he had a lighter, he could heat the key and then open the door with ease. Without thinking, I pulled a Bic lighter from my purse.

Terry gave me one of those surprised looks, without saying what he thought. Why would I have a cigarette lighter if I had given up smoking? I told him I had never had one since the night I stood on the balcony, and I think he believed me.

Terry got the car door open and turned the key to start the motor. Click, click, click-—a dead battery. He turned to me again with one of those looks without words that conveyed to me his white Datsun B210 would have started without a problem. I felt somewhat guilty. The airport service people came out and gave us a jump start. And Terry, having no ice scraper, used his American Express card to clean off the windshield, but it broke in two after he had scraped only a small space on the driver's side.

As he drove us home to our apartment, Terry hunched down just above the steering wheel to see through the small hole which grew in size as the defroster blasted away at the icy windshield. He relaxed some as we all started to thaw out. After all, my Ford had a good heater.

CHAPTER 10

Home again. Around the world, we go.

We arrived at our apartment late at night with all the car windows cleared and my Ford parked in our spot. Then we heard a hissing sound and saw steam pouring out from under the hood. My car was exhausted. I looked at my husband as he turned and smiled, not saying a word. We were home.

Aling was very excited about having a bedroom for herself, to which I could relate. But hers was much better than my first, the one I had with the Indian family. I was happy for her but had a twinge of jealousy because she was getting better breaks than I had. But that feeling soon vanished when Terry said it was time for bed. I was ready for him. We were bed-built for one another.

We made quiet love because Aling's bedroom was next to ours, not wanting her to know that we were 'messing around. To be in control, I mounted Terry knowing that he gets rather loud when he climaxes. So when we merged to the point of mutual splendor, I covered his mouth with my hand, and he just made a muffled huffing sound. Me? I could control myself.

The next day we took Aling to Park Middle School and registered her for classes. She was excited, loved school, and was always a straight-A student, even though English was her second language. Next, we were off to buy clothes for her and more for myself. I loved to shop, and my husband was proud to have two

Asian beauties holding onto his arms. As we walked along, people would second-look at us. Terry just beamed.

At this time, I started buying and hoarding sexy silk panties; they made me feel good. Over the years to come, I would buy hundreds and only wear seven of the same pair, leaving the rest to sleep in my bulging dresser drawers. Terry said I did this because I never had underwear as a child. But then he got with the program and bought me even more sexy silk panties. It was a fun game for both of us.

On occasion, I would model an extra sexy pair for him, driving him crazy for my tan, tight, body. But at times, I would decide to shut down his advances. He would call me a prick tease. I didn't know what this meant. Still, my closets were bursting with shoes, dresses, blouses, and, of course, more silk panties. I loved it!

Then I wanted a cell phone because I saw many people had one, way ahead of the rotary phone I used in Asia. And the push-button one we used on the shop wall. So, I asked Terry if I could have one. He said, "No. If a phone doesn't connect to a wall, I want nothing to do with it." After many days of my loving touch and persistence, he bought me one. Unfortunately, it had a relatively short life, because I left it on the car roof one day as we drove away.

I didn't do much better with the second one. While drinking coffee at IHOP, it slipped from my hand into the cup, and poof, it was gone. My husband didn't get angry with me, as I thought he would. Terry was so unlike my mean uncle back in the village.

As time passed, my phones would last a long time, as I learned to be more careful with them. Then Terry bought cell phones for Aling and my brothers and sisters in Asia. I was most happy to be able to talk to them whenever I wanted. Finally, he got one for himself, a flip phone which he accidentally dropped into a dirty toilet. I told him, "You have to be more careful."

Aling would come to the shop with us on her days off from school, but it was boring for her, for the most part. So we would invent things for her to do. We would have her catch flies and pay her one penny per kill. And there were plenty, because the shop was close to a feedlot. Other times we would have her stand on a milk crate and sing Asian songs. She had a lovely voice, which perhaps gave her the courage to sing the National Anthem for Coretta Scott King at Lincoln High School's packed auditorium in 1997. We were so proud of her!

We were becoming comfortable as a family. Aling was doing well in school, and Terry and I enjoyed working together. But we were in for a big change when Dr. Jack Hinze walked into our shop one afternoon. He was Terry's older cousin by ten years, and they had kept in contact since youth. He knew Terry had traveled in Asia long before he met me and had an interest in herbal medicine.

So the two got back together and decided they would travel to Kuala Lumpur and set up a business deal selling Dr. Jack's herbal products, which he made in his factory in Woodline, Iowa. Terry had already made contact with a company named Nutriherb.

They soon headed to Asia, leaving Aling and me on our own for a week. I felt abandoned because my husband and I had always stuck together like glue, plus I missed him in bed. But I knew he would make up for the lost loving with gusto when he returned home.

When they returned, I was thrilled with the news. We would be moving to Kuala Lumpur to follow through with the deal Dr. Jack made with Nutriherb. And with the apparent potential of becoming millionaires! Aling, on the other hand, was not so impressed. She liked the freedom of her American schooling.

When we received our first commission check from Dr. Jack, that gave us the money for airfare and short-time living expenses. We told Dick Carr we would be leaving the body shop and moving to Asia. He said he would miss us, as we knew we would miss him. We took most of our belongings and stored them at Terry's mother's house, and packed light. It would be easy to buy new things in Asia because money was four to one for each U.S. dollar. Terry said he was going to sell my Ford because it would just sit and wait, and for what?

When my car sold, I teared up as I watched the new owner drive it away. I glanced at Terry and saw a smile on his face. He was getting even because I guilted him into selling his white, Datsun B-210. I thought to myself, *You turd!* It was the spring of 1998, and we were airborne once again. This time, I was going home.

CHAPTER 11

THE ACCIDENT.

The plane landed in Kuala Lumpur with a heavy sigh after a long flight from the U.S. Terry waved down a taxi that took us to the same hotel in which we first made love, bringing back erotic memories for me. We got a room with two queen beds, and after Aling was fast asleep, we slid into each other's bodies with the same passion as the first time we made love, if not more.

The following day we sought out the same bellboy who stood up for us when we got married. He seemed to have all the answers. We asked him if he knew anyone that had a two-bedroom apartment for rent. He said, "Yes." He had a friend who would come to the hotel and take us to the rental. We arrived at a white twenty-five-story building called Menara Seputeh, and the man took us to the sixteenth floor. The apartment was spacious, furnished, and clean. But there wasn't any dressing table for our daughter. The landlord was more than happy to buy her one. We rented it on the spot.

The only downside was the traffic noise, which was 24/7. The city was booming, and we were willing to grow with it. At night, from our window, we would watch the traffic making noisy red streaks of light on the spaghetti-like freeways far below. We had a TV, but all the channels were in Chinese, Bahasa, or Malay. Terry did find one station that aired the show *Mash* every day at three o'clock in English with subtitles in Chinese and Bahasa. He was happy.

There was little for my husband to do. After *Nurtiherb* made the first token purchase, they would have to register the herbals with the Malaysian drug control authority. The DCA would make us rich and my husband busy. I told Terry that I wanted money to start falling like leaves from the trees. He smiled and said, I will help you rake it in.

My husband's contact was a man named Mr. Tan, who represented some very affluent and wealthy investors. One of these men owned a bank; another was the brother of a sultan, and the last was the Deputy Dean of the University of Malaysia. Money was not a problem for them, but for us, it was a different story.

We did not have much to do during the day. Sometimes Terry would take a taxi and visit Mr. Tan to see how the registration, a three-step process, was advancing. Other days, he would take the train to downtown Kuala Lumpur to buy a *USA Today* and poke an ATM for money from his credit card.

Aling and I would rollerblade down in the parking garage or swim in the pool. Sometimes we all would take the train to town and buy things we needed. But, for the most part, we stayed around the apartment and ate downstairs at the canteen. The food was inexpensive and tasty. Things, however, were beginning to get boring. I thought to myself, *I wish we had something fun to do, to fill in the time.* So I told my husband we should fly to Kuching and visit my family, some of whom he had never met. Especially my dad. But my suggestion to go home would, unfortunately, lead to a near-death experience that none of us could have seen coming.

The plane flight was short and sweet; our landing was polite, as if to welcome me back. We took the same old bus to Embrose's house, the bus in which the man tried to molest me, as I was escaping from the jungle. *Just let some bastard try that now!* I thought to myself. But the thought vanished quickly.

We arrived at his clapboard two-story house, which someone had built on the side of a hill. Half of the house was on stilts, and no one had ever painted the outside walls, so the wood sagged with a warm grayish smile. Some of my brothers and sisters were at the house when we arrived, having heard that we would be there for a few days. This get-together was a sweet and sour event because my siblings would be asking me for money. After all, as far as they were concerned, I had married a well-to-do American who was filthy rich. Little did they know we were living off Terry's credit cards.

My sister Jaming cooked up a feast with all of my favorite jungle foods. Everybody sat in a circle on the floor because there wasn't a table. We all ate with our hands, except Terry, who didn't like touching food except for hamburgers or pizza. So my sister found him a fork and handed it to him with a puzzled expression on her face. Terry sat there with his shirt off exposing his white skin, a stark contrast to our very tan bodies.

That night he and I slept in the same upstairs bedroom as before with the single light bulb hanging from the ceiling and no curtains or glass in the window. Aling slept on the floor near her grandfather. Outside, the noise level seemed worse than before. Motorcycles roared past, sounding like chainsaws on steroids as they sped by, cutting the silence into ribbons. Or was I getting spoiled by living in America?

Aling had heard of McDonald's but had never been to one, and Terry was crazy for some hands-on food. So that morning, we crossed the water-filled creek on the footbridge. The bus to Kuching would be coming in a few minutes. There were other people already waiting so we formed a line along the edge of the highway.

We heard the clank and rattle of the bus; and could see it was close. I turned to my husband and told him to get ready to board so we could get a good seat quickly. He was facing me and couldn't see the oncoming traffic. I looked past his head and saw a speeding car skidding out of control behind the bus, trying to avoid a rear-end collision. It was heading towards Terry, but I didn't have time to warn him; it was all happening much too quickly.

The car hit him in the small of his back, rocketing him into the nearby creek. The car was relentless, following him down into the creek bed as it turned over and the roof crushing my husband down into the water.

I could not see Terry. I thought he was dead under the car, my partner, my lover, my hope for the future. Then, from under the overturned car, he pulled himself free with one hand and crawled over to the bank. He tried to stand but collapsed to the ground. His left foot was twisted to the side, and his head, hands, and butt were bleeding. The weight of the car had frozen his right arm into an angled shape. The car hit so hard it knocked him out of his shoes, marking the point of contact on the ground beside me.

A young man, also waiting for the bus, ran down the embankment, and lifted Terry from the ground. He then carried him up and over to the front of Embrose's house and laid him on the ground. My dad, who was out front, sat down cross-legged and cradled Terry's head in his lap as my husband was shaking uncontrollably.

Aling rushed to his side and asked, "Dad? Are you alright?" Terry looked at her and said, "I think I'm going to pass out." With tears forming in her eyes, Aling thought he said he was going to die. The poor girl, believing she was losing the only dad she would ever have, started to have a panic attack. I was just happy to see that he was still alive.

There wasn't any emergency 911 number to call, but lucky for us a white van stopped to see if we needed help. Two young men dressed in white got out and said they were employees at a clinic ten miles down the road. They helped my husband into the van, which was oddly bare of any medical supplies. After we drove off, Terry lay on the floor and tried to talk with me, but his teeth were chattering so much he was hard to understand.

But I understood when he said, "Watch this." He grabbed hold of his frozen-angled arm and, with an audible 'pop,' snapped it back into place. He smiled at me, and I knew he would be alright, but for how long?

We arrived at the clinic, and the charge nurse looked surprised when we got out of the van. Nobody had ever done that before as it turned out they used this vehicle only to haul the dead off to mortuaries. Things went fast because the staff all wanted to go home at closing time, which was noon on Saturdays. My husband was soaking wet and shirtless from the accident, and his tan shorts were torn open in the rear, exposing his white butt. They helped him onto a gurney and pushed him into a small room.

A Chinese doctor entered without fanfare and pressed both of his hands very hard on Terry's chest to check for any broken ribs.

Terry let out a loud groan. I thought to myself, if he didn't have any before, he would now.

Next, the doctor examined his leg without the benefit of an X-ray. He pulled and twisted both his leg and foot, and then, without wiping the wet grass debris from Terry's leg, he slapped on a crude white cast, tightly pinching his toes together. Still, Terry's head, hands, and butt were bleeding.

A nurse shaved around the gash in his head, making it bleed even more. Then she stitched it up without any anesthetic. I could tell Terry was very uncomfortable. The nurse then asked him to turn over so she could sew up his butt cheek. He said, "No, it will heal by itself." The nurse ignored the scrapes and cuts on his hands.

Then I heard the closing of doors and the clicking of light switches since it was now time to go. I told the nurse I had to get my husband some dry clothes. She said, "Please hurry. It's time for us to close." I ran to a nearby open-air market and bought him a shirt, shorts, and a pair of flip-flops.

When I got back, my husband was standing and leaning against the nurse's desk without a crutch, which would have been helpful. I changed his shorts in front of the nurse and put on his shirt. Terry could only use one flip-flop.

With his teeth still chattering, he asked if there was any charge? When the nurse said, "No," he looked at her with surprise, smiled, and said, "Thank you." She then handed him some pills to take, without saying what they were for. Terry never took any.

A taxi was out front waiting for us. My husband lay down in the back seat for the ride back to Embrose's house. Within a few miles, Terry puked on the floor of the taxi. I rolled down the window to let the stink out. By now, his chattering had stopped. We arrived at Embrose's house. As Embrose and Aling helped Terry out of the car, I handed the taxi driver the fare and gave him a large tip.

Terry hobbled across the footbridge with me holding on to him; he looked terrible. My family thought they would never see him again. Terry will soon be out of the picture. I thought to myself, "Do I now only have half a man?"

I could tell he felt as helpless as a caged tiger who was not even able to pace and forth. All he could do was sit. When the sun went down, his world got even smaller. He would hobble to the doorway and stare into the darkness outside with a sad look upon his face.

I did my best to help him by giving him sponge baths, which I liked to do. And I cooked him rice and eggs, which he liked very much. I even trimmed the bottom of his cast to free up his toes so that he could wiggle them. On the second night, I helped him up the stairs so we could sleep in our bedroom.

I wanted to know if my man was still a man. I started to undress him, but he knew what I wanted. He started complaining his back hurt, and his head, and so on. But that did not stop me. I knew what I wanted, and I was going to get it. As I made his penis as hard as a diving board, I mounted him and began to move up and down slowly. Yes, Terry was still a man, and he was my man.

And the weeks passed by slowly. When Terry started feeling better, we booked passage back to Kuala Lumpur. I decided to take my father back with us since he had never been on a plane or anywhere in his whole life. After we boarded the plane, I noticed how funny Terry looked dragging his cast down the narrow aisle. My father looked scared as he walked down the aisle behind Terry, so I held his hand. He looked at me and smiled.

The landing was very polite, which I was grateful for since my father was still very uneasy. We took a taxi back to the apartment and settled in. We were still waiting on NutriHerb, which seemed unending. Were they going to give us the deal? I was getting scared about money since we were now living totally on credit cards.

As time passed, I took my father to the zoo, where he saw his first elephant. On a different occasion, Terry and I took him to a bar where the dancing girls were scantily dressed. His eyes widened in wonderment. The music was so loud I knew my father could hear it, even though he was nearly deaf. He could feel what he couldn't hear on the floor, in his chair, and the vibrations in the air. I looked over at my father. He had a smile on his face and a Guinness Stout in his hand, as did I. In fact, to this day, I always drink one Guinness Stout on my father's birthday in his honor.

Six months would pass. To our despair, Nutri-Herb did not pan out. Our golden egg had failed to hatch. After hearing the news, we looked at one another and teared up. We bottomed out. But Aling was happy. She would now not have to go to school in Kuala Lumpur. So, using our credit card again, we bought a ticket for my father back to Kuching and arranged for the family to pick him up. As we helped my father board his plane, Terry pulled out his card again to purchase tickets for Aling and us to return to the states. Thank God for American Express.

CHAPTER 12

More 'Travels with Terry.'

The years passed quickly, although the seasons dragged on, especially winter when I was utterly miserable. But I would torture Terry in bed at night with my frozen feet. He would not complain, but I could feel him brace himself against the typical warmth of my body. Spring came, and I was happy for the most part, working with Terry at our body shop and having some control over our future. We were living in a nice apartment. Aling was doing well in school, had a good job, and had saved enough money to buy a car. Terry and I were getting along well, and business was good, but the paint fumes were beginning to wear us down health-wise and sapping our energy. It was time for a break.

So we decided to take a trip with Aling as a reward after she graduated from high school. We would first fly to London for a few days, then on to Bombay for a few more, then complete our trip by arriving at my family's home in Kuching. We bought our tickets the day before we were to leave, but there was a small problem. Aling told us she would meet us in Kuching, because she couldn't get away from her job any sooner--her employers needed, she said, at least a week's notice ahead of time. I felt terrible that we had not included her in our original plan, but I said okay and told her to change her ticket. She dropped us at the airport the next day, and Terry and I flew off for our new adventure.

We landed with an uncomfortable thud in London then found a hotel within walking distance of the airport. The place was well-worn, yet we were surprised by how expensive our lodgings turned out to be.

I wanted to call Aling to find out if she had any trouble getting her ticket changed. I called through the hotel switchboard but had a difficult time understanding the operator. His thick English accent frustrated me, but we were finally able to get through to Aling. She picked up on the first ring, so I asked her if she could get her ticket changed? Then came her surprise!

She blurted out, "No. I'm not coming." There was a slight pause in her voice. Then she said, "I got married instead!" I couldn't believe my ears. I said, "To who?!" She replied, "To the boy who took me to my prom. You remember, he came over to ask Terry is he could take his daughter to the prom." I was livid! Would this guy turn into another Hee Ping! I slammed the phone down, looked at Terry, and screamed, "She got married!" Like me, he, too, was livid.

But, after a while, we both calmed down; we looked at each other and came to the same conclusion. Aling was now of age, a grown-up, and she could choose her direction in life, regardless of what we thought or felt. By the time we returned from our travels, Aling had moved to Chicago with her new husband. They were now a couple, and they would have to figure out things for themselves.

The next day, after Aling's phone call, we took a tour around London. We enjoyed seeing the highlights, but the fog and rain dampened my spirits. And after the recent news, I think I was still in shock. It was hard for me to come to grips with the fact that my only child had decided that she didn't feel she could tell me she wanted to get married. I already felt guilty about having been absent until she was twelve years old, but once she was living with me and Terry, I had done everything I could to make her feel loved, and cared for. As to exactly why she had chosen to hide her relationship from me and Terry.

Between being jet-lagged, tired from travel, and stunned by this earth-shaking development, I felt like I needed healing, in the warmth of an Asian climate, like what we would experience in Bombay, the city now called Mumbai.

We got up and ate breakfast at the hotel in the morning while Terry looked over our tickets. He told me we had plenty of time to catch our flight out of London. Terry always took control of our schedules, and I always trusted him with them. After finishing our eggs and toast, tea and crumpets, we leisurely walked to the airport, where we expected to get our boarding passes. When we got there, we found the airport nearly vacant except for one agent behind the counter.

Terry handed her the tickets and said, "Boy, we must be pretty early." But she glared at us and said, "No! You're just very late!" I gave Terry a stern look. The agent looked at her computer and told us the plane had already boarded, but if we could move fast, she could still probably find us seats. We were lucky we only had carry-on luggage. We followed her at a fast pace, whizzed down the jetway to the plane's door, and with a slam of the door, we quickly found our seats near the front of the aircraft. My glare went away as I looked around and realized we were seated in the comfort of first class, ready to be spoiled by the accommodations reserved for the wealthy. At the same time, though, I realized I would never again trust my husband with our ticket reservations or boarding times.

It was a nine-hour flight. Yet we enjoyed the wide seats, legroom, and outstanding service compared to what we got in economy class. This first-class experience now spoiled me, and in my heart, I truly forgave my husband for his mistake. The plane landed with a punctuated skid of the tires. Then we deplaned before the economy class passengers, which made me feel positively uppity. We got into a taxi and told the driver to take us to an above-average hotel downtown. He spoke good English and said, "I will take you to a nice three-star hotel." But, as it turned out, it was only a three faint-star hotel.

The room reeked of stale cigarette smoke and alcohol. The blue shag carpet from the 1960s was as dry as a wheat field in Nebraska before harvest; it went crunch, crunch, crunch, as we walked across it. There were multiple cigarette burns on the carpet, bed cover, and end table where smokers left to smolder the remains of their addiction as they passed out drunk. The room was a fire trap, and we were on the sixth floor, too high to jump to safety in the event of a fire. For the first time in my life, I felt disgusted that I, too, had been a smoker.

We were exhausted from the flight and tried to settle into our musty room. I was thirsty but afraid of drinking water from the bathroom faucet for fear of it being contaminated. I told Terry to call down for the bellboy to bring up some bottled water, which he soon did along with three large bottles of beer for Terry.

I took the first shower, and Terry soon followed. We got into bed with trepidation. When I reached up and pulled the string to shut off the light above our bed, sparks flew across the ceiling, followed by the smell of burned wire. That was it. I wanted out of this room, so Terry called down to the front desk, telling them what had happened and that we wanted another room!

A bellboy appeared at our door; he apologetically took us to another room, this time on the third floor, which was like the first room, but it was not that as far to jump in case of fire. I had a hard time getting to sleep that first night in Bombay. So I snuggled close to my husband for comfort, hoping the new day would bring us fun and adventure. Such was not the case.

The following day, as we pushed open the hotel's front doors, hot, foul churning air from the unpaved dirt street outside swept into our faces. As we stood there and watched the traffic go by--tuk-tuks, cars, bicycles, people, and the occasional cow--it was almost impossible to breathe.

That's when I saw, across the street, a family of four, all of whom were sitting on the ground, cross-legged with their backs against a dilapidated concrete wall. Two boys, similar in appearance and from what I could tell, around four years old, were seated on the dirt barefooted,. Beside them was a girl, also poorly dressed, who looked about ten. As soon as the mother saw my husband and me, she pushed the little girl toward us to beg. Darting between the traffic with skill, she crossed the street and stopped in front of Terry with her hand out, saying nothing but displaying a sad, pleading look upon her face. She reminded me of myself years ago, poor, with only one dress and no shoes.

I felt so lucky to be far away from my past, but the girl touched my heart. Feeling sorry for what the poor child was going through, I gasped and began to cry. I then jabbed my husband twice with my elbow. He knew what I wanted him to do. He dug into his pocket and pulled out some rupees, and handed them to the small girl. She said nothing, did not smile or nod, but turned and ran back across the street. Her job for today was over. But not for tomorrow. We would be under her surveillance.

Then, with a wave, Terry flagged down a tuk-tuk, and I told the driver to take us to the center of town. The man grunted to us in crudely spoken English, then began to dart off through the congested traffic filled with the pungent odors of Bombay invading our senses. At one brief stop, out of nowhere, a little naked boy, dirty and with the biggest, hollow dark eyes I had ever seen, ran up to us with his hands cupped in front of him. He was no older than five. Terry quickly grabbed his camera and took a picture. The tuk-tuk driver turned and gave my husband a shaming look.

I tried to give the poor boy some money, but we quickly sped off into the flow of traffic. My eyes stayed fixed upon the boy's as we drove away. He got nothing but dust and specks of dried cow dung that floated in the air like dandelion fuzz.

After a half-hour ride, we found ourselves downtown. Terry generously tipped the driver; I did not wince as I had often done before. Looking about, I noticed many wooden shanties and stores selling fruit and cheap clothing. I thought, *This is downtown?* Then I turned and looked at what appeared to be the center of this downtown area, a tall glass and steel monument of a building that would not have looked out of place in a big U.S. city. We slowly made our way through the crowds toward the building and went inside. Clean, with modern decor, this building seemed totally out of place.

At first, an overly friendly salesman hesitated to greet us, but soon he was standing in front Terry, speaking English with what I recognized as a cultured Indian accent, trying to sell us rugs, then jewelry. The carpets did not interest me, but when he showed me a gold necklace, I knew it was for me, mine at first sight.

When I asked Terry if I could have it, he winced and jokingly said, "Well, it would look good on an Egyptian Pharoah's wife," as he pointed to the price tag. As he reached for his American Express card, my husband did not skip a beat and told the salesman we'd take it. I was so happy I threw my arms around Terry and kissed him. But then I realized what we had done. I was afraid to wear the necklace here in Bombay, fearful someone might run up and grab it from my neck.

The grateful salesman got us down another tuk-tuk, then bid us farewell. When we arrived at our hotel, the family of four was still sitting across the street. The little girl's attention perked up when she spotted us. Within moments she was standing in front of us, with the same sorrowful expression on her face. Once again, Terry handed her more rupees. That night we stayed in our room and ate junk food from the vending machines downstairs, avoiding a third encounter with the young waif across the street from our hotel.

The following morning, I looked out the window down to a nearby lot covered with green grass, where I saw a man squatting in the grass with a pair of scissors in his hand. The thin brown man wore nothing more than a pair of dirty tan shorts. And there he sat snipping away at the grass with his scissors, snip, snip, snip. It was a strange sight, and his performance went on like this for hours, that day, and day after day, for the duration of our stay in Bombay. And it seemed as though he would never finish his endless task. Sometimes, I felt the same way about my life.

We were bored and felt trapped by the little girl, her mother, and her two brothers, who sat waiting and watching for us across from our hotel. I felt sorry for them, and as I said, I related very much to the little girl. Even so, I didn't like her confronting my husband. He was not tough enough to say no. Like the man snipping grass, begging was what she did, hour after hour, day after day.

Still, I wanted again to go shopping, this time for a pair of shoes to match my purple dress. When we ventured out that morning, we discovered the family had vanished for the time being. So we took off walking unhindered, but not for long.

From one shop to the next, we roamed the streets of West Bombay. Finally, we arrived at *Metro Shoes*. I found a pair of purple shoes to match my dress. I put them on, and they seemed to fit reasonably well, so I wore them out of the store. The saleslady put my old shoes in a big white bag that said in bold red letters, 'Metro--More shoes to choose!' But, I only wore those shoes on that one day, never again. For some reason, they hurt my feet.

As we crossed a street, we passed by another hotel, and then, from out of nowhere, a group of about a dozen little ragamuffins pushed me aside and surrounded Terry. They grabbed hold of him, yelling, "Rupees, rupees!" My husband was trapped, and it seemed, about to be robbed, or worse. But then, a big Indian man, hearing all the commotion, came out of the hotel and began swatting all the children, getting them to stop.

While standing by my side, the man pointed at my husband and shouted, "You. Run! Now!" As Terry ran off, the man began giving me a lecture about having a white guy with me on the streets. My being brown, he told me, wasn't much of a problem. But when it came to Terry, a white guy with money, it was an entirely different story. This kind man walked with me until I saw Terry waiting for me a few blocks up the street.

My husband thanked the man for his help, and we then took a tuk-tuk back to our hotel, where the girl was once more waiting for us. Terry gave her money yet again.

I looked out the window the following morning, and sure enough, the thin brown man was still at his job cutting the grass, snip, snip, snip. Again we dared to venture outside but saw no trace of the family across the street. This time we took a tuk-tuk to another part of town, hoping it would be safer.

Not to our surprise, another young girl, perhaps ten years old, approached us as we made our way down the crowded street. She wore a multi-colored skirt and blouse with a maroon sari that was draped over one shoulder. She looked very stylish and clean, yet had no shoes or sandals upon her feet. Her clothes were not very new, but she spoke excellent English, when she said in a sweet voice, "Would you like for me to show you around town? My name is Aashi." We later learned her name meant 'beautiful smile,' which she had.

Aashi was very personable, so I asked her how she learned English so well. She replied, I grew up in an orphanage that had a school. She made such a good impression on Terry and me that we would have taken her to America in a heartbeat, if possible. She never asked us for any money, but instead, we just followed Aashi as she began leading us down the streets of Bombay.

As we wandered about with our young tour guide, many beggars of all ages came up to us. Aashi would fend them off in a stern but polite manner using their language. After a while, she asked me if I would like to see where some of her friends lived. I said yes, thinking of the orphanage, which I soon found was not the case.

We walked to the rocky coastline of the Arabian sea, which was not far away. The first thing we saw was a group of people cleaning themselves, and others defecating in the surf. Many of these people were bent, crooked, or deformed, with missing limbs, and some had faces that reminded me of "The Elephant Man," a movie Terry had taken me to see back in the states. Several of these people came up to us, but Aashi pushed them away. Except for one, who turned out to be a friend of hers.

He was a young boy about the age of twelve and very lean. I was surprised when he came up behind my husband and began running his hands up and down Terry's body, including his face. I thought this was odd and turned to Aashi with a curious look. She told Terry to stand still. "Don't be afraid, he won't hurt you. He is blind, and this is the way he gets to know someone. He has never 'seen' a white person before, and he is curious. Terry did not move, and when the boy had finished 'looking' at my husband, we shook his hand. Aahsi said, "This is my friend, Rahul." She then spoke to him in their language and told him our names. He smiled at us and shook our hands again.

After we left Rahul at the beach, Aashi stayed with us on our walk back to our hotel. When we arrived, the family across the street chose not to bother us, I was sure because they saw our 'tour guide.' Perhaps they had crossed paths with her before, and Aashi, too, had hurried them away.

Terry took a picture of Aashi and me, which I still have today. I then told him to give her a generous tip even though she had never asked for any money. We thanked her for spending time with us, and with her beautiful smile, Aashi bid us farewell, then ran off down the street.

Aashi, too, had reminded me of myself when I was her age. I was a young girl trapped by circumstances, with little control over what happened to me, yet still survived a somewhat difficult childhood. I still wonder what happened to Aashi. She had so much potential. After Terry and I had returned to our room, I went over to the window and looked down at the lonely man below in the grass, still snipping away with his scissors, snip, snip, snip. Sadly, like Aashi's, his story was like so many others, never-ending stories of poverty, starvation, poor health, and little hope for the future.

Terry and Pedo's 'tour guide' while in Bombay, India, a young girl who spoke excellent English and who Terry and Pedo would have adopted 'in a heartbeat.'

We didn't like staying in our room, so Terry went downstairs and asked the bellboy for ideas. He told us we could take a taxi to Bollywood, India's version of Hollywood. He said he would have an air-conditioned cab waiting for us shortly before noon. We didn't like getting up early for anything if we could help it. That night Terry and I made slow and quiet love to help fill the time in our room.

The following day we took our time in the morning, showering and washing off our lovemaking glow from the night before. I got dressed, and then I went over to the window before we left the room. There was the grass cutter, snipping away, snip, snip, snip. He had moved about three feet from the day before, snip, snip, snip. Later that morning, our taxi arrived, and we were ready for our Bollywood trip. The bellboy met us downstairs and opened the hotel's doors and then the doors to the taxi. For some reason, Terry forgot to tip him for his help. I thought to myself, *I hope this won't throw a curse on us for our future adventures in Bombay.*

As we sat down in the back seat, the driver welcomed us in English, "Hello, hello. Good day."

Terry told him, "We would like to see Bollywood, " and the driver smiled and said, in an enthusiastic voice, "Yes, yes. I will take you there."

While we headed for Bollywood, we saw the coastline fly by us on our left. Then my husband noticed what appeared to be a massive dump, which seemed to go on mile after mile. He tapped the driver on the shoulder and said, That sure is a big dump, while pointing out the window. The taxi driver turned his head and looked both of us in the eyes in a serious manner, and said, No. That's where many of our people live. Without realizing it, my husband had embarrassed me so much that I took my fingernails and dug them into his bare arm, leaving impressions that lasted for over a week.

Not long after, we arrived in Bollywood and walked around for a little bit while the taxi driver waited for us. We were sadly not very impressed. And, as it turned out, our hearts were not into it. We went back to the taxi and told the driver, "Please take us back to the hotel." It seemed like a much longer ride than before. The once pleasant driver was now as silent as we were, as we made the journey back to Bombay.

After he dropped us off in front of the hotel, we were both famished from our solemn and dismal ride. We also wanted to avoid the young beggar girl who had taken advantage of us far too many times. We had already seen enough heartbreaking things for one day. Instead, we found the back door of the hotel and started walking down the alley. Within two blocks, we passed a dumpster in which we saw three half-naked children digging through the trash. When they saw us looking at them, they smiled. Terry went for his camera, but I made him put it down. Like the tuk-tuk driver, I did not feel comfortable about him taking pictures of impoverished children.

Leaving the alley, we got back on the sidewalk, and soon I spotted a restaurant and bar called On the Rocks. It looked clean, so we went inside. The waiter, who was also the owner, spoke excellent English. We both ordered a fish dinner; I had bottled water, and Terry, of course, had a beer. The food was delicious, filling, and just right for me. I was full, but my husband wanted to have a second helping, and so, he ordered it.

But, as they say, his eyes were bigger than his stomach. He could only eat about half of this second meal, so he waved the waiter over to the table for the check.

"What are you going to do with your leftovers?" the waiter asked. Terry replied with a smile, "Leave it on my plate." The man then went ballistic and, unable to control himself, confronted Terry, saying, "Don't you realize we have so many starving people here in India? And here you are, a rich American, who could care less. You feel it's okay to waste food. To have me throw it away? Shame on you!"

Terry, chastened said, "I'm so sorry. I will take it with me. Could we please have a small box to put it in?" The waiter soon returned with the leftovers neatly wrapped in a brown paper package with a white string around it.

We slowly got up, thanking the man for the beautiful meal. We looked out the front door and saw that the coast was clear. We did not see the little girl or her family anywhere. We darted for our hotel, and suddenly, the little girl jumped out from behind a tree in front of Terry. Instead of rupees, Terry handed her the package of leftovers; she smiled and then ran off.

By now, both Terry and I had just about had enough of Bombay. Yet, there were still a few days left from our seven-day adventure. We decided to stay in our musty room and not do much of anything. We watched the old scissor man outside continue to cut the grass, snip, snip, snip. By now, though, we were both so sad and fed-up by our experiences here, our sex life was even out of the picture. Nothing seemed to be going as planned. I wondered idly if Terry's failure to tip the bellboy before our Bollywood trip had triggered this curse?

By the seventh day, Terry and I had decided to cancel going to Kuching since Aling wouldn't be there. I called my family and told them not to expect us. We had had enough travel for the time being and too many crazy people to deal with. I looked forward to the calm and safety of our Nebraskan home and our return to the good old USA. After Terry had scheduled our departure flight for later that night. The bellboy had picked up on our despair and said he wanted to help out. He told us he had a friend with a car who would be happy to give us a ride to the airport and said he would like to ride along with us if it was okay. We agreed on the plan.

As it turned out, it was a long dark ride across town as we made our way to the airport. But during the trip, the bellboy and his friend got into a terrific argument. The two men argued loudly back and forth in a language neither of us understood. As we continued, it seemed to me we had driven past the city and then out into the outskirts of Bombay. Here there were no lights except for the shacks lit by flickering candles in the windows.

A thought suddenly popped into my head. Maybe we were about to be kidnapped, robbed, and then killed. A gradual sense of fear melted down over my body. I tightened my grip on my handbag into which I had placed my gold necklace the day before. No one would have ever guessed I'd hidden it there. Or maybe someone had found out. I reached for Terry's hand and squeezed it tightly. We looked into each other's eyes in tacit agreement that we didn't know where we were going. Was the bellboy's friend taking us toward the airport? Or someplace else? We were scared. The driver and the bellboy continued to argue, shouting at times. But what bothered me most was when the driver kept looking at me through the rearview mirror with what appeared to me to be a smirk upon his face. Was I about to be raped by him before being killed?

Then, as my fear was about to overcome me, the airport lights came into view, confirming that yes, we were heading in the direction of the airport. My fears subsided. Terry and I looked into each other's eyes with a sigh of relief. The car stopped, and they let us off in front of the airport. Terry reached into his pockets and gave them all the rupees he could find. As we walked away with our carry-ons, I glanced back at the car, and I could see the two men were still arguing. I was feeling somewhat better until we entered the airport.

Once inside, we became aware of several heavily armed soldiers roaming around the airport. It wasn't very comforting to me to see all of these men with rifles in hand moving about with unsmiling faces. I looked at one of these men with my best girly smile and said, "Hello." But I didn't get any positive response: just a serious, no-nonsense look in his eyes. We still had another hour before boarding time, and there were only two unoccupied seats left to sit on in the waiting area, so we took them.

Directly behind us, an Indian woman was coughing and spraying bits of spittle on the back of our heads. I thought to myself, *What if we come down with some horrible disease?* Then they announced our flight would soon be boarding. So we got up and went through security, where two or three of the armed soldiers were standing about and watching everyone as they carefully passed through the two lines for baggage inspection and the metal detector machines.

We found our gate and boarded our plane. There were hordes of people who came after us, and as we stored our carry-on baggage in the overhead compartments, I saw, to my dismay, that the coughing, spray lady was sitting directly behind us. We would be doomed for the next several hours to endure the spray of her bacteria-ridden wet spittle.

After this risky health encounter, we continued with many short stop-over flights and boarded our final flight to America from Taiwan, headed for LAX in Los Angeles. From there, we flew to

THE HEADHUNTER'S GRANDDAUGHTER

Omaha and found our waiting car, an Ford Taurus belonging to me, then drove back to our body shop in Eagle, Nebraska. But we had to work hard and save money to refresh and pay off our American Express Credit Card account. Afterward, we would once again be looking forward to our next adventure, once more in Bangkok. We were chasing time, and it was moving almost too fast. I had turned forty, and Terry was now fifty-one.

As the years went by, Aling was no longer a part of our everyday life because she and her husband Matt had relocated to Illinois. At first, there was scant communication between us for the next several months. Then things began to change, mainly because of her three blessings, which would shift Terry and my life for years to come filling the empty corners of our lives. It was December 2000, and our daughter was having difficulty keeping her life in order, living in Chicago.

CHAPTER 13

WHAT A WONDERFUL WORLD IT IS

I was starting to become increasingly aware that time was passing and we were not getting any younger. The paint fumes in the shop were getting to the both of us, especially Terry. He started having panic attacks in the middle of the night that scared me, because I didn't know what to do for him.

Whenever this happened and I asked him how I could help him, he'd say, "Just go back to sleep. I can handle it," and he would go downstairs. I was worried about him, and could hear him pacing for hours around the shop. Finally, I don't know just how much later, he would come back to bed. I could never get to sleep until I felt his warm body beside me again. It seemed the shop was pushing us both out.

I told my husband it was time for a trip. When we first met, he asked me to travel the world with him. So now I called him on it. Once he agreed to take a trip, I asked him where he thought we should go.

Instead of giving me a real answer, he asked me if I would like to take a long train ride, not like the short one we took from Singapore to Kuala Lumpur, but this time to Bangkok. That was where we met after our three-month separation while he was getting paperwork done for me in the U.S. and I was still in Borneo. Remembering our first, very passionate nights together made my inner thighs quiver and tingle with sudden desire. When I had recovered myself, I knew just what to say: "Book it!"

A week later, we were off to the airport in Omaha. Terry drove his old brown and tan VW van and left it in long-term parking. I never liked that van because I could not drive a stick shift, and it had a bed in the back into which Terry was always trying to get me to play with him in one of his 'on the-spot' fantasies. I told him that would never happen. He never succeeded; the bed remained a virgin.

When we boarded the plane I didn't feel my usual fear of flying. Still, I wouldn't say I liked the tight seating arrangements in economy class, and I wistfully remembered how, years before, the gate agent in London had upgraded us to first class on our flight to Bombay. But that thought disappeared with the closing of the cabin door. The flights that followed were relatively smooth, except for the landing in Singapore. The plane slammed down on the runway so hard that some overhead compartments popped open, causing luggage to spill out. The pilot's voice came over the intercom apologizing for the rough landing, and we arrived at our gate soon after.

It was late at night, so we took a taxi to the Copthorne King's Hotel, where we had a reservation. It was a long, dark ride, and the Chinese driver kept threatened to doze off to sleep, regardless of the irritating meter chime that would go off every few seconds. Both Terry and I kept talking to him, trying to keep him awake and prevent an accident. I spoke to him in Chinese, and Terry did so in English.

It was hard to think of what to say to keep him awake, but somehow we managed to keep him replying to us, in both languages, which kept him awake long enough to get us to the hotel. We both were relieved when we arrived at the hotel without mishap, and Terry gave him a modest tip in U.S. currency.

We got a room and showered together; I was exhausted, but not Terry. I lay down in bed, expecting to make love before going to sleep. Terry surprised me when he said, "Pedo, I need to move around some. I'm not ready for bed." And with that, he got dressed and then announced he was going down to the lobby.

I stayed in bed watching the time tick by. Minutes became an hour. I was worried and began to wonder if anything had happened to my husband. Did some hooker grab him and seduce him away from me? Or maybe some kidnappers, seeing a rich white man, took him for ransom? My mind raced with thoughts of all the bad things that could have happened. I was worried. Then, there was a light knock on the door, and I heard Terry's voice in a hushed whisper. "Pedo, it's me. Open the door." I jumped from the bed and opened the door.

There stood my husband with a gold and blue heart-shaped compact with a small mirror in it. He had brought back a present for me from the hotel's gift shop. He was my man, kind, generous, and thoughtful. That night I gave him a bit of heaven in bed.

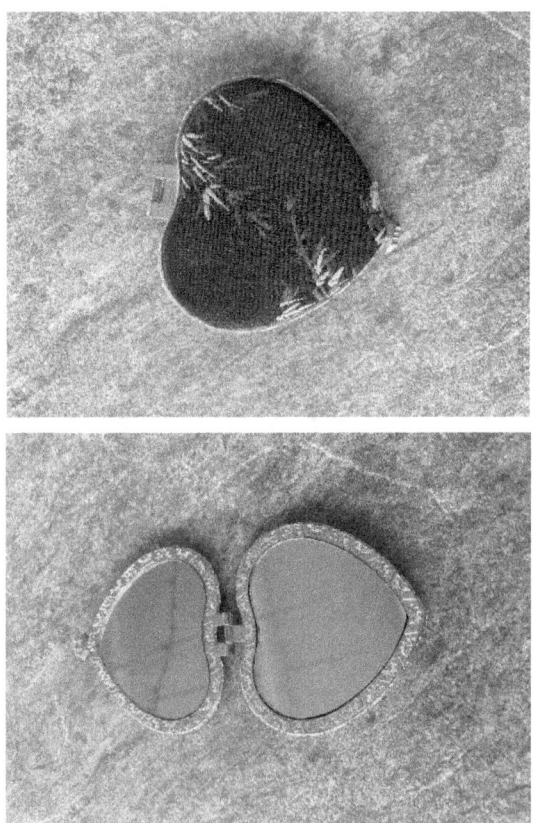

Above is a photo of a compact which Terry bought for her in Singapore.

We had planned to get a taxi to the Keretapi Tanah Melayu train station in the morning, but we were pleasantly surprised when the bellboy told us it was within walking distance. That was a relief, after our terrifying taxi ride the night before. Within a few minutes' walk, we arrived at the station, a large gray concrete building, where a professional photographer was taking pictures of an attractive, tall Chinese fashion model, using the building as a backdrop. As Terry stood behind and beside the photographer, he decided to take photographs of her too. I didn't mind; my husband could look all he wanted at other women as long as he didn't touch them. If looking at an attractive model started a fire within him, I'm the woman who would end up fanning the flames into a roaring blaze of passion.

We went to the ticket counter and bought two round-trip tickets to Bangkok, first-class; it was inexpensive! Once aboard the train, we sat down in the sitting/seating car. The train was an antique by American standards and would have been in a museum back in the states. But we could see it was well-maintained.

As we sat down, I noticed a small table between us. We talked while glancing out the side window at the hubbub of the station. Then the train whistle tooted, the train jerked forward, and we were off on a new adventure. As the train picked up speed, a couple came down the narrow aisle while holding on to the backs of each seat to steady themselves. They sat down across from us.

To me, they looked like husband and wife. They spoke in German with a broad, heavy accent. Terry turned to the man and said, "Hello," with a smile. But, the man didn't even look at Terry. Instead, he snubbed him and turned his head away from us.

My mind went back to the German man I was a pen pal with and wondered if he had the same snooty manner in public. I mentioned it to Terry, but I could tell he was jealous of any man from my past, so I dropped the subject. At that point, we both felt uncomfortable, so we moved to another seat.

It was near dark when the supper bell rang, and people began to drift towards the dining car. To get there, we had to cross the gap between train cars through a black, segmented passage that moved with a slow, twisting motion. I felt a bit unsettled as I rocked back and forth as if I was crossing over the metallic floor of some elaborate moving funhouse. My stomach began to feel a bit queasy.

Once in the dining car, we sat down to a simple meal and enjoyed ourselves despite our brief walk of disequilibrium in the funhouse passageways. But then, seeing our reflections in the dark glass windows, I felt content and at peace, rolling along steadily through the Malaysian jungles toward Thailand.

Late afternoon faded into the night; it had been a long day. Terry and I went to the sleeper car, not knowing what to expect. Which funhouse room was ahead of us now? The beds were small, akin to a single sleeping bag. There were two berths on each side of the car, an upper and lower with a thin white curtain covering each bed, to offer the veneer of privacy. For a person to get into the upper berth, the porter would provide a short wooden ladder.

The porter sensed our attraction for one another and said, "I'm sorry, but you cannot sleep together. It would be best if you stayed in your bed." I took this as a challenge. I wanted to be with my man. I climbed into the lower berth and squirmed out of my clothes down to my panties and bra. Terry climbed up into his bed without using the ladder. I could hear the zipper as he removed his jeans, and then, I assumed his T-shirt. I could see the outline of his body above me, pressing down through the mattress of the small bed above. But I had to wait. It seemed like hours when finally, the porter shut off the coach lights except for the ones at the far ends of the sleeping car.

Now it was our time. With my foot, I poked at Terry's butt above me. Without words, he knew what I wanted and was more than willing to give of himself. He silently slid down from above without the aid of the ladder, parted the thin curtain, then slide in beside me like a snake.

Like sardines in a can, side by side, edge on edge, his front to my back, we removed our underwear with some effort and care. With one hand, he unsnapped my bra. To my surprise, I wondered how he pulled that off? How many girls had he practiced that on before me, to be so smooth and clever with his hand? A tinge of jealousy arose in me, but my mind cleared as he entered me from behind swiftly, satisfying our mutual craving. As I began to moan, he gently covered my mouth with the palm of his hand. After we climaxed and settled, he gave me a light kiss on the back of my neck, then climbed up into his bed.

Lying in my bed, I listened to the train as it moved slowly through the jungle. The slow, steady sound of crickets and the occasional cry of a bird made me homesick for my grandfather and my memorable time together when I lived with him. I closed my eyes and listened to the song of the train wheels rolling over the tracks, click-click, click-click, as it lulled me to sleep.

We got up early the following day because everyone else did. I nearly had a fit as I struggled to get dressed in such a cramped space, as I'm sure Terry was doing the same above me. It was breakfast time, so we headed to the dining car, having to cross the metal funhouse floor between each car. The noise and the smell of diesel locomotive exhaust pierced my senses as I carefully took each step as I moved slowly over the rocking, twisting motion of the steel plates between cars.

We sat facing one another at a small table. I glanced out the side window as the green jungle raced before my eyes in a blur. Lost in my thoughts about my past and future, which collided at times, I was awakened by the porter's voice, "What would you like for breakfast, madame?"

Without looking at the menu, I said, "Rice and eggs." My mind had instantly snapped back to the present. "And the same for my husband, please," as I smiled and looked at Terry. But I forgot to order us coffee. The porter had caught me off guard. Terry smiled, "No worries," he said, as he reached into his small bag, "We always carry bottled water."

After breakfast, we went back to the sitting car to enjoy the ride. Shortly, we heard the "toot, toot" sound from the locomotive at the front of the train, and we noticed the train beginning to slow down. It came to a stop at a station of a small village, where some passengers boarded while others got off. The conductor smiled and said, "Attention, please. Our visit here will be brief, so we suggest you stay on board rather than getting off to check out the scenery."

Terry opened our window to let in some fresh air, and within seconds, the banana lady appeared before us. The image of Corporal Maxwell Klinger from an episode of the television show *M.A.S.H.* suddenly came to mind, and at the same time, a smile crossed Terry's face as I caught his eye. As we came to know each other better over the years, we discovered that often we came up with the same thought simultaneously without words.

She had a basket of bananas balanced on her head, as did Corporal Klinger in *M.A.S.H.* Terry held up two fingers, and the lady gave him two bananas. He gave her a ten Ringgit note which was worth about five dollars. Instead of giving him some change, and without any eye contact, she turned and took off, running down the side of the train with her colorful long skirt flowing behind her and one hand holding her banana basket onto her head. With a frown on my face, I looked at Terry and thought to myself, *When will he ever learn about my country?*

But, he redeemed himself when a small, shoeless bare-chested boy of six came hurrying down the aisle. He stopped in front of Terry, offering old soup cans filled with black coffee. My husband dug into his pocket and gave the boy his loose change. The boy, in turn, handed us coffee, smiled, then darted away. I smiled at Terry. It was a fair exchange. We now had our breakfast coffee.

As I put my lips on the rough edge of the coffee can, sipping its warmth, a smile grew inside of me and tickled my thoughts. I bet that was the banana lady's son.

The train tooted twice, and with a jolt, we were off, moving down the tracks toward Butterworth, Malaysia, near the border of Thailand.

Above, we are at one of the many stops during the train trip from Kuala Lumpur to Bangkok, Thailand.

We had a two-hour layover in Butterworth, so we decided to walk around outside the station. Behind the depot, I noticed an Indian man sleeping on the ground next to a luggage pushcart. He was naked except for a pair of dirty shorts. To my surprise, I noticed his brown dong hanging down below his cutoff shorts. It was as flaccid as he appeared to be. I elbowed Terry to look, which he did. We smiled at each other with slight chuckles, which turned into sighs.

Walking around to the front of the depot, we saw a young, beautiful Asian girl who was perhaps about eighteen. It seemed that she was trying to sell herself in a unique way, by wearing a tight white T-shirt with the words **Fuck Me** written in bold black letters across the front. Her ample breasts and firm nipples punctuated the 'F' and the 'E.' To complement the advertisement, she wore tight black shorts. My husband's eyes just about fell out his head as he gazed at this bold and forthright young girl. At first, I was somewhat angry with this girl's reckless behavior. But I decided to withhold my judgment, realizing that we all have to make a living somehow, working with whatever means we may have. I grabbed my husband's hand and pulled him in the direction of the ferry we were about to board, heading to George Town, the capital of Penang, Malaysia.

We had time to spend, so we boarded the ferry, which crossed over to Penang Island and George Town, Malaysia's third most populous city with 708,127 inhabitants as of 2010. It was a slow two-mile trip across the Penang Strait of the Andaman Sea, part of the Indian Ocean.

We stepped off the ferry when we arrived but didn't wander too far from the dock for fear of missing the train to Bangkok. Finding a small store nearby, we went inside, looking around, and stepped into the music section. Terry spotted a cassette tape by Louis Armstrong, picked it up, and showed it to me. He said, "Do you know who this is?" I said, "Of course I do! Louis Armstrong. My boss at the salon would often play cassettes by English-speaking singers on his stereo to entice and make foreign customers feel at home.

Terry bought the Louis Armstrong cassette for me, which I still have today, but technology has advanced far beyond the days of playing music on a stereo cassette player. We boarded the ferry again, leaned on the rail above deck and watched the water churn below us.

I recalled that my boss at the beauty parlor played his favorite Louis Armstrong song repeatedly almost every day, "What a Wonderful World." I looked at my husband and smiled and thought to myself, "Yes. What a wonderful world it is."

CHAPTER 14

THE CLASSIC PLACE AND BANGKOK BAD

As we stepped off the ferry back in Butterworth, we heard the train whistle telling us it was time to board. We ran to our train car, holding out our tickets for the waiting conductor. He smiled at me and, with a sweep of his hand, ushered us aboard. Finding two empty seats in the sitting car, we sat down and waited for the train to start. Within a few minutes, the train tooted, jolted, and rattled, and with a deep inhalation of the diesel engine we were off to Bangkok, several hours away.

There wasn't much to do except sit and look at one another, other than occasional glances of the green jungle whizzing by, which was pleasing at first but could only go so far. So I took out a deck of Aviator playing cards from my purse that a stewardess had given me during one of our long flights from the U.S. I wanted to play 'Go Fish,' as I did when Aling was a child. But Terry only knew how to play gin rummy, which his grandfather had taught him as a child. I then said, "Let's play 'Twenty-One,' and showed him how. After a few hands, he gave up and said, "No, I don't want to do this." He gave up because I could add up the numbers faster than him. Sometimes, Terry was so hard in the head. Caving to him, we started to play the slow, methodical game of rummy. As before, I won most of the time, then finally, as before, he became frustrated and said, "I don't want to play anymore." What a cop-out.

While still in the sitting car, I looked through my reflection in the window and watched the lush green Thai jungle pass on the other side of the train. As the train began to take a turn, I saw the long length of the cars in front. That's when I caught a glimpse of a porter throwing garbage from the train into my pristine jungle paradise. The sight of such a heedless act on his part made me heartsick. I could only imagine what the monkeys thought of such a disgusting gesture on his part.

The constant clicking rhythm of the rails began to slow its tempo as we neared the outskirts of Bangkok. As I looked out my window, I saw another peculiar sight. Hundreds of multi-colored shirts, pants, and sheets draped the crushed rock along both sides of the train. It seemed as if the material had melted before my eyes, conforming to the rocky surface in the hot sun. Here was Bangkok's open-air laundromat with free deodorizing furnished by the diesel fuel and creosote fumes from our passing train.

The train continued at its slower pace, and then, as we approached a colossal structure, the cars seemed to inch their way into a vast railroad station. The architects had designed the roof over this massive building using curved steel beams, which supported a honeycomb of glass that reminded me of the inside of a giant beehive. It looked as though a giant cataract had formed over the glass ceiling, caused over the years by the massive amount of soot that rose from the trains coming and going beneath it.

Before our train had come to a complete stop, Terry stood up and took our luggage down from the webbed overhead bin. Then, a young boy with determined dark eyes darted aboard the train and grabbed our luggage without saying a word. We had no time to yell, "No, wait a second." Having no other choice, we jumped up from our seats, following the boy's preplanned strategy to a parked taxi out in front of the station. The boy then stood holding the rear door open with a wide, toothy grin. Our luggage was sitting near the open trunk. I grinned at the boy in compliance, and as he had anticipated, Terry and I got into the back of the taxi. The boy closed the door, and through the open window, my husband handed him a small tip. As soon as our luggage was in the trunk, we heard the slam of the trunk's lid. I turned to see the boy disappear into the noise of the crowd.

The taxi driver spoke some English, and Terry said we wanted to go to a 'high level' hotel while lifting his hand upward. After our Bombay incident and the firetrap room, we wanted the best in Bangkok. The driver said, "You want to go to a fancy hotel?" Both Terry and I nodded our approval, and off we went into the heavily congested streets.

When I first met Terry seven years ago in Bangkok after we were married, then separated for three months, I didn't realize how big, dirty, and dangerous the city could be. We mainly hung out around our hotel and stayed in our room. And in so doing, proved, over and over again, our love and lust for one another. I have no regrets. But this time, I wanted to explore Bangkok and venture out of our bedroom and into the city itself. My husband was game for my idea. But as it turned out, I had a tense time in the beginning.

The fancy hotel seemed to be miles away and through many traffic lights. And due to leaving the train so fast, I didn't have time to use the restroom, and I had to pee urgently. I told Terry, and he asked the driver to pull into a gas station. He said he would if he got a chance. The minutes seemed like hours. The traffic was bumper to bumper, and drivers would ignore the stoplights, forcing themselves through the intersections. It seemed endless. I looked at my husband's watch, and twenty minutes had passed since the last stoplight. I was about to wet myself, and Terry told me to pee on the taxi floor. The driver heard this and bravely inched ahead, breaking the flow of traffic. Within a few minutes, the driver pulled into a gas station, and like a bolt of lightning, I ran into the not-so-clean toilet and relieved myself without losing my dignity. From that moment on, my husband and I used this experience to gauge how badly we needed a restroom. "Bangkok Bad" was the worst.

We arrived at a hotel called the 'Classic Place,' which, from all appearances, seemed exceptional. It was, however, quite different from the Grace Hotel, which we had stayed in years before, with glass encaged girl boys and girl prostitutes for rent on a lower floor. And our room was better furnished, quieter, and very clean. But of course, then, our focus was mainly on our bed, a pleasant memory for me, and of course, for my husband. This time around, however, I wanted to explore the city with him.

We had a pleasant first night in our room and enjoyed a satisfying complimentary breakfast in the morning. Afterward, we met Onanong Sriponnok, a beautiful young girl who had a travel agency desk down in the lobby. She had jet black hair, piercing dark eyes, and spoke excellent English. We liked her instantly. Onanong made plans for us the next day to tour the city with her as our guide. After the Bombay incident, when a group of street urchins mobbed my husband, I wanted someone to be with us who could speak the Thai language and keep us safe.

But that first night, when we were on our own, we walked only a few blocks from the hotel for fear of getting lost. The streets and sidewalks were dark, dirty, and filled with turmoil. Cars and taxis would honk their relentless warnings as if their horns gave them power. At first, it seemed we could blend into the crowd flowing along uninhibited, but then it became clear that Terry's white face was a sure target for prostitutes and beggars. I tried to fend them off for him. But he's such a nice guy, and at times weak, and easy to trick into giving away his money.

Anyway, as we were moving down the street, we saw the strangest thing. There, in the front of a store outside, we could see a huge elephant. I had never seen one before, and standing beside the elephant were two sexy Thai girls trying to usher people inside the store to buy things. Terry stared at the two girls and smiled. I couldn't blame him; after all, he's only a man. For a few cents, we bought some green bananas from the owner of the pachyderm. I held them up to the elephant, and he took them from my hand with his long, wet nose. His trunk frightened me a bit, but then he put the bananas into his mouth with a graceful sweeping curl of his trunk. Here was one more new experience for me.

As we continued to walk down the sidewalk, the foot traffic began to let up, and we found an outdoor restaurant that looked interesting, so we sat down. The waiter came, and I ordered clams, and Terry just wanted a beer. At times, my husband could be a picky eater.

It was fun to sit and watch the people cross back and forth in front of us. It was almost like watching a movie happening right before our eyes. We stayed there until the sun went down behind the buildings.

As night was approaching, we strolled back to 'he Classic Place holding hands and enjoying each other's company without having to say anything. When we arrived, Terry, the gentleman that he is, opened the door for me, and together we walked to the elevator. But before we could push the up button, a skinny hotel security guard stopped us, then confronted my husband. Using hand gestures, the uniformed security guard pointed at me and then shook his head with disapproval. In this manner, he told my husband he could not take me up to his room. Terry told him, many times, that we were married, but the man did not understand English. Then, we pointed to our wedding bands, and he grimaced, showing us his embarrassment. He raised his hands in the air and gestured for us to continue on our way. The guard held his hands together as the elevator door opened and gave us a slight bow in apology.

The guard thought I was a lady of the night. I admit I sometimes dress provocatively; if you've got it, then why not flaunt it; Terry didn't mind. That same guard made the same mistake a couple more times while we were there, but finally, he recognized us as the couple we were. To him, all white guys looked alike, at least until he took a closer look.

The following day Onanong was at her desk waiting to take us on our tour around Bangkok. We first boarded a ferry that snaked through the city on the Chao Phraya River. I leaned against the railing and saw the surface littered with garbage. I turned to Onanong and was about to point this out, saying, "The river is disgusting." But I thought better of it and kept silent. After all, it was her country, and I don't control that problem, only myself and my mouth.

Then a Buddhist monk dressed in an orange robe with a shaved head wedged himself in between Onanong and me. I felt uncomfortable when I noticed his side glances going up and down my body. Perhaps he was one with himself, and for a brief moment, had let go of his celibacy, at least in his mind. After all, he was a young man in his prime. I then gave him a sideways glance and moved closer to my husband.

We soon disembarked the ferry and walked to the Temple of the Golden Buddha. Onanong looked at how I was dressed and said, "I should have pre-warned you. One must dress conservatively in places of worship." I agreed with her, so we went to a small clothes shop, and Terry bought me a pair of jeans and a black T-shirt that said, "Bangkok."

Before entering the Temple, we had to remove our shoes out of respect. But I was worried about Terry's expensive Reeboks, thinking that someone less honest than most might exchange them for their cheap flip-flops. We came upon a sizeable disorganized pile of various types of shoes out in front of the Temple entranceway.

We stepped inside, then bowed down to the solid gold 5.5 ton sitting Buddha. It was enormous. We then bought and lit some incense for an offering. I briefly touched the solid gold necklace I was wearing, which Terry had bought me in Bombay. There was no comparison between my necklace and this colossal statue of the Buddha. But I could not hold that against Terry. After all, he was only a mere mortal.

We bowed again as we left the temple, stepping out front to retrieve our footwear. And just as I had feared, my husband's Reebok sandals were gone. I was angry, as was Ononong. All she could say was, "Sometimes it happens. We, mortals, are flawed and sometimes cannot be trusted." I told Terry to "pick another pair of shoes, and let's get out of here." But he didn't want to put his feet into someone else's dirty shoes.

My temper cooled down as we walked back to the store, where I bought my shirt and jeans. Terry sprinted ahead. The pavement was so hot it burned his bare feet. We told him we would meet him there. He bought a pair of cheap pink-and-green flowered flip-flops with orange soles and smiled at me. "Next time, we'll let them steal these instead."

The next stop along our tour was The Temple of the Reclining Buddha. Again, we left our shoes out front and went inside, bowed in reverence before a giant golden Buddha, who was lying in unruffled repose staring at the ceiling above, or perhaps toward heaven?

We dropped coins into one of the 108 bronze bowls that lined the temple walls for an offering here. As the coins fell, they made a nice ringing sound. Both of these temples were impressive, but after visiting them we felt like we had seen enough. We bowed once again before we left the temple and then went outside to get our shoes. And sure enough, Terry's pink and green flip-flops were still there waiting for him.

We took the same ferry back to The Classic Place. This time the amorous monk was nowhere to be seen. We paid Onanong with a thank you and a generous tip, then headed back to the elevator where, yes, the skinny guard stopped us once again, even though I had was dressed appropriately this time. Perhaps this was his only purpose, to show what little power he had regarding this job. After he recognized us, he smiled, clasped his hands before him, and bowed once again, giving us free use of the elevator. Once in our room, we showered then made tender love, realizing we just needed to be with each other, once again. Without any sideshows. Just us.

We stayed around the hotel for the next few days or ate at nearby sidewalk cafes. The time was approaching for us to catch the train back to Singapore, and our cash was running short. The following morning it was time for us to head back. Terry calculated how much of his remaining cash we would need for food, taxi, and train fare. All we had left was a single one-hundred-dollar bill, which he could take to a money changer for 3,280 Bhat, more than enough to cover those expenses and get us back to Singapore. After that, Terry would use his credit card for our hotel bill and such. But when he gave the one-hundred-dollar bill to the money changer, the man said he wouldn't take it because someone had taken an ink pen and put a mustache under Benjamin Franklin's nose.

What were we to do now? The only person we knew was Ononong. So we went to see her, showing her the defaced bill. She said the money exchangers here were very picky with U.S. currency but said she could help us. She took the bill, left the hotel, and returned within one hour, with much fewer Bhat than we expected.

But at least we had travel money now. We were grateful for her assistance and thanked her.

The following day, as we stepped out of the elevator with our bags, before us stood the skinny Security Guard. He smiled, bowed to us, and said something in Thai. We assumed he was saying goodbye, but we would never know. Onanong was sitting at her desk but stood up when she saw us coming. I gave her a farewell hug. My husband hugged her, too, and also placed a kiss on her cheek. I didn't know whether to be jealous, angry, or what, so I just let it go. The one thing I did know was when I'd first met Terry years ago; I could tell he was a lady's man. The main thing he had to remember was he was my lady's man.

There was a taxi out front, so we put our bags and ourselves in the back seat. Terry said two words, "Train station," and off we went. This time the traffic was moving smoothly, a great improvement from when we first came from the opposite direction. We arrived at the station in good time, and there was no little boy to greet us with a smile. Terry tipped the driver, and we went inside to buy our train tickets. This time we decided to reserve a private sleeping compartment, which was much better than before and, to our surprise, cheaper. It was a bit awkward though, to be in a moving bedroom.

The train was off with a jolt. Knowing that we would be traveling for hours, the thrill of rail travel was beginning to get a little boring. But that changed when we got to the Thailand / Malaysia border. I remember how, when we were traveling from Malaysia to Thailand and our train had gotten to the boarder, the passengers jumped off the train and rushed toward the wooden immigration shack wanting to be the first to get their passports stamped. There was a lot of confusion. When Terry handed the agent our passports, the man glanced at them, stamping Terry's, but for some reason, not mine. In hindsight, neither of us caught this at the time.

This time around, when Terry handed the agent our passports, the agent looked at them both and gave Terry's back to him after stamping it. But he kept mine in his hand, looked at us both and said, "Follow me to the main office." Fortunately, it was not far from where we were. We entered another building where a large man sat behind a desk with armed, unsmiling men who must have been guards, standing on either side of him.

The man at the desk was a really big guy, and when we were in front of him he looked at me and said, in English, "Where is the stamp on your passport?" I told him that it should have been there, as there was on my husband's, but for no reason we knew of, the border agent didn't stamp mine when we came through the first time.

At that moment, I heard the train outside sounding its whistle, warning of its imminent departure. So I did the only thing I could think of. I smiled at the big guy and showed him my wedding band.

He pressed his lips together, and his forehead wrinkled as he said, "Eh, mph." Then he looked at me, smiled, and stamped my passport, letting us go to board our train.

At times the smile of a pretty woman can go a long way. Once we were on the train, the conductor told us that many young women from Bangkok often try to jump the border for work in Singapore. The big man was just doing his job.

We still had a few more hours and one more immigration checkpoint to pass before entering Singapore. It went smoothly. But that was only a reprieve from my immigration problems. We arrived at night, walked hand in hand back to the Copthorne King's Hotel, where we started. The next day we would fly home to the United States. Hopefully, the flights would be smooth, which they were. The turbulence came after our landing in Los Angeles.

Arriving in the U.S., I had mixed emotions as we entered the LAX terminal. One part of me was happy to be home; the other was afraid to go through immigration because if something were wrong with my Malaysian passport or green card, they would send me back to Malaysia. We followed the multicultural stream of individuals that snaked up to the gates like a crowded Walmart check-out line on a Friday after payday. I inhaled deeply; it was our turn.

Terry handed the young officer our documents; he looked at me with his soul-piercing blue eyes that seemed to evaluate people in a split second. Once again, he looked at my husband's passport and stamped it, handing it back to him. He looked at me again and, without a blink, raised his arm in the air. I Immediately two officers, a man and a woman escorted us away. My heart sank. I thought, "Are they going to send me back to Malaysia? Would my husband follow me?" We were scared; they took us to a seemingly empty part of LAX and told Terry to wait somewhere else.

As they started escorting me away, Terry spoke up, saying, "My wife's English isn't very good. Can I go with her?" They said, "No! Wait here."

The officers put me in a large room where many Muslim men and women, dressed in traditional attire, were seated on chairs along the walls. I thought they must be there because of 9/11 some years ago. But, I was not Muslim; I was just Pedo. I waited for more than an hour, hoping Terry was okay. Then an officer called my name.

I went up to the window and stood; there was no chair for me to sit in. I saw the officer had my passport and green card. He asked me many questions about where I had been and for how long. I was confused and scared, so much so that I could only give vague, fuzzy answers. Then he came to the point. The birthdate on my green card and the one on my passport didn't match, which neither Terry nor I had ever noticed.

He then said, "You'd better get this fixed, or you will have more trouble in the future." He stamped my passport and pushed the documents through the slot at the bottom of the window, and then another agent escorted me back to Terry. When we saw one another, we both teared up. We hugged.

We did fix the problem, but it took a year and turned out to be expensive.

The root of the problem was I never had a birthdate on my birth certificate, only the month and year. When making my passport in Malaysia, I just randomly picked November 1st. In the U.S.A., when we applied for my green card, for some reason we picked November 15th, having forgotten that there was a different birthdate on my passport.

CHAPTER 15

A New Beginning

When we got back from Bangkok we had to knuckle down. Money was tight, and we were borrowing from Peter to pay Paul. But I trusted my husband with money, hoping he would never prove me wrong.

It was starting to get cold as fall was upon us. I reflected on my first arrival in Nebraska on a frigid January day. I got goosebumps. The time of year had come again to gather food to feed the monster, our custom-built, steel wood-burning stove that Dick Carr had made for us to heat our spacious shop. Its mouth was big enough to swallow a railroad tie whole, and it had an insatiable appetite. If it had had teeth, it could have bitten your arm off during feeding time. Only Terry got to feed it.

The monster also served a dual purpose. The stove kept my husband and me warm in the winter and it cleared dead wood year-round from Dick's property of which he had acres abound. It was heaven for Terry because he loved cutting trees with a chainsaw that reminded him of the ear-splitting motorcycles he hated so much. He was hard to figure out at times.

I wouldn't say I liked cutting firewood, but I did appreciate the benefits of a warm stove in the winter. I would go with my husband and help him load lengths of wood into his old white Chevrolet pickup, which Terry had beaten up over the years, but it had an excellent heater, like our warm stove. After we got back to our building, I would stack the cut wood nicely in the shop next to the 'Monster.'

Winter came, and finding dry wood in the snow difficult. My feet, hands, and butt froze. After going inside the shop, I would back up slowly to the glowing hot stove to warm myself. Then I would take a hot shower, go upstairs, and slip into bed with my husband. If my feet were still cold, I would warm them on my one-hundred-and-forty-five-pound personal foot-warmer. Sometimes Terry would be a brat and start complaining. Whenever he did that, I would remind him that he was the one who brought me here, and soon he would settle down.

I could hardly wait for spring and to get back to my large garden next to the shop. The soil was dark brown and fertile, and in it, I grew many different vegetables. People told me I had a green thumb. And I believed I did. I spent hours in my garden touching the green leaves, silently communicating with them. When I did that, I felt at peace.

Then, the big wind came, what the people around here called a tornado. My husband stood petrified in fear, and while I didn't see anything of concern, the fact that Terry was so frightened made me feel scared too. It was just wind. We stood at the shop door holding hands and watching small debris fly about, skipping across the asphalt parking lot. As we heard a ripping sound of metal and looked at the tall grain silo across from our shop, I could feel his grip tighten on my hand. Then, unbelievably, the top of the silo broke free and sailed across the sky, as if a giant invisible hippie had tossed it, like a large frisbee, into the air. It was out of sight within seconds.

Now I knew Terry had a reason to be scared. He would often tell me that not having a basement below our shop for when storms like this one appeared without warning was a problem. So, instead, we got into the white Chevrolet pickup and drove down to the local bar, which did have a basement.

When we got there, there were no customers inside. The only brave soul there was the barmaid, who was happy to see us arrive. I told Terry to get a beer for himself and a Coke for me. The barmaid looked at Terry with grateful eyes and said, "No charge."

We stood there with our drinks in hand and looked outside through the aluminum-framed glass doors onto an empty street. The tornado sirens went off, wailing their terrifying warning. We could hear them blasting into our ears since they were only one block away. The wind stopped, the air was silent, and I got an eerie feeling in my stomach. BOOM! The wind picked up again with a pent-up vengeance. The aluminum framed bar doors began to rattle, threatening to blast open, so Terry and I went over and grabbed the door handles, hoping to hold them tight. The barmaid rushed to our side and locked both doors from the inside but said, "We need to move away; the glass might shatter!"

Now we were all terrified. I glanced out the windows and saw the tops of trees bending over and kissing the ground. Snap, snap, snap! The trees fell to the ground. Two of them were blown out of sight by the gale -force wind.

The building was quivering, as large hailstones beat like a fierce toneless drum upon the roof. The safest place was us to be was in the basement. But instead of retreating to the basement we ran and crouched behind the heavy wooden bar with the barmaid. I believe we were all so interested in watching Mother Nature showing off her strength and power before us mere humans that our curiosity overruled our desire to stay safe. It was indeed fascinating to me, yet terrifying, too.

Then, with no warning, the wind was gone, and the sky cleared, the savage storm ended as suddenly as it had started. The tornado siren sounded all clear. We thanked the barmaid and went outside. The birds chirped frantically, looking for their nests and families in the downed trees. We looked at my husband's pickup, which was pockmarked all over with hail damage. I thought to myself, I bet he repairs it. After all, we own a body shop. Yet, for whatever reason, we never did.

When we got back to the shop, we discovered it hadn't suffered any damage. The silo across from us was, though, badly damaged, and there were tree branches scattered all over. We were both tired and went to bed but did not sleep well. The following day, we turned on the TV and found out that the F4 storm--the second most powerful rating for a tornado--had completely destroyed the small neighboring town of Denton. The tornado had killed one person, injured thirty-eight more, and would cause, in the end, $160 million in property damage. The only thing left standing was the bank's steel vault. We had been just on the outskirts of that twister. On May 22, 2004, I gained some respect for what Mother Nature was capable of doing with a wild, wind storm.

The seasons continued to change, but what didn't was the health hazard of paint fumes in our body shop. Both Terry and I were beginning to feel unwell because of it. He would get goofy, especially after painting, even though he wore a respirator. I came down with a chronic cough, and my skin was as dry as an autumn leaf.

Terry was sick and tired of working in the body shop. I liked the money, but I knew he was feeling guilty about me having to get dirty. In his heart, he believed bodywork was a man's job. I remembered a moment, after first getting to the U.S., Terry looked at me and said, "All you have to do now is sit behind my desk and look pretty."

Of course, he was wrong. There was no way I could sit on my butt doing nothing all day. Over the years I told him this many times, but I think he still felt guilty on some level, because in his heart he felt it was a man's responsibility to earn money, and a woman's responsibility to take care of her man.

Trying to break free from the shop, Terry decided to look for another job and do bodywork only on his days off. If he did get another job, it meant that he would be gone all day, five days a week, leaving me alone for eight hours at a stretch, and that prospect didn't thrill me.

Terry applied for a job at the Lincoln Regional Center, a locked-down facility that housed people with mental health problems. Terry had had years of experience in this field before he met me, so he got the job in a heartbeat. But when he thought about having to leave me alone all day, after all was said and done, he once again chose to inhale the fumes of freedom. And working for himself, and us being together. Terry turned the job down and decided to be my man 24/7. I loved him for it.

We continued working hard and enjoying each other's company. But, each month, we were greeted with our credit card bills, a ritual I was not too fond of. Terry could only make the minimum payments, so that put a damper on any future overseas travels, at least for the time being. But because of my cooking skills, using one burner on a green propane camping stove, we ate well and stayed healthy, aside from the paint fumes. I had been used to cooking on an outdoor wood fire when I was younger.

All in all, it didn't take much to make me happy. The only thing that ever caused friction between me and Terry was my passion to buying new articles of clothing, which was one thing that Terry would feed into along the way.

My early life, when I worked with my uncle and had no underwear had made a lasting impression on me. Buying clothes seemed to help me with that shameful fear.

We went along keeping our heads barely above water and getting dosed by the toxic fumes. Then, one afternoon, the phone rang, and my husband picked it up, "Hello." While he leaned against the wall, he played with the spiraled cord attached to the bottom of the wall phone.

On the other end, his good friend Dr. Jack was asking him to move to Tucson, Arizona. He was starting up a Naturopathic Clinic and wondered if we might like to work for him. He asked Terry to think about it and to figure out how much salary we would need to get by each month.

Terry hung up, came over to me as I was sanding one of the cars, and asked me if I wanted to move to Tucson and work for Dr. Jack. It didn't take me long to think it over: no dirty hands, no wood-burning monster to feed, no toxic fumes to breathe, and sunshine year-round. What could be better? What could go wrong? I said, "Yes!"

Terry called him back within a few minutes with the money figures in mind and our answer of "Yes!" Without a pause in his voice, Terry said, "See you in Tucson."

We rented a U-Haul trailer and hooked it up to our green 1996 green Jeep Grand Cherokee, which I had picked out from a car salvage auction. We had rebuilt it and gotten it in good running order. It was faithful and ran well.

It didn't take long to load up the trailer. We took along a few bodywork tools and our clothes, mostly mine. And, of course, the queen-sized mattress we had just bought from Mattress Firm in Lincoln, which still had the new smell. As my husband cut off the tags, I looked at him with curiosity wondering why he would do that to something new. I was going to ask, but let it go.

We said our goodbyes to Dick and Joe Carr, which was emotional for all of us. Then we pulled out and drove across U.S. Highway 34 to Casey's gas station and filled our tank. Terry and I got back in the Jeep, closed the doors, looked at one another, smiled, and said goodbye to Nebraska. Terry didn't see me do it, but I knocked three times on the side of my head for good luck. We then pulled out onto the highway toward our new adventure. I could feel my Jeep sigh with the weight of the trailer, a new job for her, and the same for us. I looked at the blue sky above as the puffy white clouds moved through it over my head. It was the beginning of spring 2005.

CHAPTER 16

Exciting People

We were fifty miles from Tucson, as the sun was coming up greeting us with a beautiful sunrise. It made me feel warm and welcome. Perhaps it was a sign of good things to come? I was tired from us both driving all night. I snuggled back into my soft seat and loosened my seatbelt a bit. I closed my eyes and fell into a deep sleep with the steady rhythm of my Jeep's engine, which gradually turned into the sounds of my jungle, the birds, the monkeys, and the insects. And the smell of burning coals.

I was ten years old, and it was very early in the morning. I was getting the fire ready for coffee. I would get up before my grandfather and uncle, the only real time I had for myself. I squatted and stirred the embers from last night's fire with a short stick. When the red coals blinked awake, staring at me, I stared back, and threw the stick into the fire to feed them. Glancing upward, I saw the sunrise painting the sky in hues of red, orange, and yellow as it pushed the night away. My jungle was green again, and I was mesmerized, at one with myself, peaceful and still. Then came my uncle's shrill voice, "Where's my coffee!"

I woke up abruptly as if my seat belt had tightened against me somehow all by itself. Terry reached over and placed his hand upon my leg, giving it a gentle squeeze. "Hey," he said. "Wake up. Have you been dreaming? It seemed as though you were fighting with someone."

"No," I said. "I'm okay." I didn't want to get into it. For the most part, I retained that peaceful, still feeling. It had been a good dream, until my uncle came into the picture.

We finally made our way into Tucson and what appeared to be civilization. We were both exhausted. In hindsight, it was a bad idea to drive 1,200 miles non-stop.

I pointed to an exit and told my husband, "There. Let's get off on Grant." Over time, Terry had gotten used to me telling him how to drive and where to go, so he took the exit ramp. Our goal was to find a house near the clinic, which made sense. Finding the clinic was easy for me since I had the address on a piece of paper in my hand and had already checked directions from the highway to it. It didn't take us long to get there from the interstate, and when we arrived, the building was locked up, waiting for us to open it for business.

I looked at Terry, and I could see he was as tired as me, as was my Jeep. I could tell. But now we needed to find a house to rent, that day if possible. A big job, a big town, and little time to do so.

Pulling the U-Haul trailer behind us was a hassle while trying to find a place to live. Terry had to make sure he didn't get trapped on a dead-end street or in some parking area. Backing up without jack-knifing the trailer would be a difficult trick.

So we drove very slowly around one street after the next, looking for "for rent" signs. Late that afternoon, I spotted a sign in front of a four-bedroom house, which of course, was too big for us. And it was starting to get dark. I noticed a tall palm tree in the front yard, surrounded by many green plants and flowers in planters.

"That's it," I said, "That's the house I want." In an exhausted voice, Terry replied, "Any port in a storm."

Sometimes he would say things I didn't understand, and I would ask him to explain. But before I had a chance, he took his cell phone from his pocket and dialed the number on the sign. I understood that meant, "Yes."

Within a few minutes, a young man and his wife showed up. We struck a deal for a month-to-month lease. The couple helped us move in then and there. We were home, at least for now.

The following day we met Dr. Jack and his wife Dianna at the clinic, and we laid out a plan. Terry was to go around to other doctor's offices to promote Dr. Jack's DRX spinal decompression machine, which could also allow thermal imaging for breast screening. My job would be to take phone calls and assist him with running the DRX.

But the business was slow, and months went by without many patients, and we were getting worried, as were Dr. Jack and his wife. We had lots of downtime. I kept busy gardening while Terry studied a used anatomy book Dr. Jack had given him.

At times we would walk down the alley together to a liquor store that sold different beers from all over the world. My husband liked Polish beer the best.

Since the clinic was not doing well, Dr. Jack already had a plan B ready to go. He was friends with another Naturopath named Dr. Nelson, who had an established practice in Palm Desert, California, and we were welcome to join him.

We rented a U-Haul trailer again and loaded our meager belongings into it. By now, my Jeep was used to pulling a U-Haul trailer, so we'd been down this road before. While loading it up, I swore it was the same one we had used before. But Terry said, "They all look alike." So I dropped the subject. However, the DRX machine had to have special handling, so Dr. Jack hired a bonded private company to move it.

Lucky for us, the journey to Palm Desert, California, was only a day-long trip. I had never been to California before, so my husband clued me in on the state. Lots of palm trees, temperate weather, and fascinating people.

As we neared the city, I looked at the outside temperature gauge above the mirror, flashing red, warning me that something wasn't right. If my 'girl' had a tongue, she would have been panting for air.

I turned to Terry and gave him one of my best impertinent looks. He could be so mistaken when it came to some things. He kept a straight face and didn't say a word. He was right about the palm trees and, as it turned out, about the weather, he had missed the mark. The thermometer above the mirror read 125 degrees Fahrenheit.

Dianna surprised us by renting a house, which made our transition to our new home much easier. However, the downside was a long drive to get to the clinic and the Hy-Vee grocery store for food and Terry's beer. The worst part for me was I had no place to plant a garden. I hoped that my green thumb wasn't going to wilt.

We took a couple of days off to settle in before going to the new clinic. The first night we were both exhausted and only kissed each other with the anticipation of making love the next night. By then, I would be more than ready for my man.

The second night we went to bed later than usual, falling asleep in each other's arms, forgetting about the unfulfilled promise we had made the night before. Then I had a vivid dream that I was making love to my man. I woke up wet and touched his manhood to wake him and said quietly, "Can you take me now?"

In one slow breath, he entered me fully. As my body gave way to the splendor, the bed began to shake, pictures fell from the walls. And then I experienced one of the best orgasms I have ever had.

I naturally felt and thought my man was good at fulfilling my sexual needs, but not *that* good! We felt tremors under our bare feet as we got out of bed. The shivering house was making groaning sounds, unlike the ones we had made making love.

Soon everything became calm, and we hung the pictures back on the walls. We crawled back into bed, startled by the vibrations in the house and ground that we had just felt. But, for a long time, I lay in bed wide awake and couldn't fall back to sleep.

The following morning, we found out that earthquakes were frequent in Palm Desert because the city was situated right on the San Andreas Fault line. I'm sure, however, in Terry's head, his lovemaking technique had helped make the bed shake and me quiver and quake in sheer ecstasy.

After getting dressed and eating a quick breakfast, we made the hour-long drive to our new place of employment. Dr. Jack and his wife Dianna would join us in a few weeks. We met Dr. Nelson, a tall, lean man with white hair. He was also surprisingly a chain smoker, which struck me as odd, being somebody I believed to be in the practice of improving one's health and well-being.

The constant smell of tobacco and smoke gave me an overall queasy feeling about working there, along with making my clothes stink. It was also very uncomfortable when Dr. Nelson chose to discipline us like children whenever we walked down the halls if we made noise dragging our heels." Making my way about the clinic in high heels was not easy to put up with all day long. The good Dr. Nelson proved, in my opinion, to be nothing more than a quirky and somewhat eccentric older man.

Being chastised by Dr. Nelson was one thing, along with doing thermal scans or treating people on the DRX machine. Terry would help him with his patients.

Dr. Nelson would put his hand on Terry's shoulder, and he would then put his other hand on the patient's shoulder, thereby transferring my husband's energy to them. Terry, of course, had his doubts about this practice working, but at times when he came out of the exam room, Terry would find himself physically and emotionally drained. So some kind of transfer was happening, hopefully for the good of the patient.

However, I did not understand this day-to-day routine, nor did I like it. My husband's abundance of strength and energy was supposed to be for taking care of me. Not everyone else!

After several weeks I began to feel in my heart that this clinic wasn't going to work out for me, let alone for Terry. Fortunately for both of us, Dr. Jack decided that he needed his own clinic, which was soon to come.

But before the door closed in Palm Desert, my husband and I had a never-to-happen-again surprise confirming two of his projections about life in California. As I mentioned before, Terry was right about the palm trees, wrong about the weather, but correct in his observation that we would meet exciting people there.

We were getting ready to do a thermal scan image on a thirty-year old woman who had stomach problems. When she came into the imaging room, she wore a tight white T-shirt without a bra. I looked at Terry and knew that he, like me, had noticed her hard, firm nipples, which clearly pushed against her white T-shirt. As I had done with other patients, I asked her to unsnap her jeans and lift the front of her T-shirt to expose her belly button.

She looked at both of us and said, "Would you mind if I remove all my clothes?"

"No, that's all right," I said as I glanced at my husband with a straight face.

Her breasts were in full bloom, with not a hint of sag in either one. But as we looked at the thermal scan, we could tell that her breasts had implants. They showed up the color blue in the image. No heat. This woman just wanted to show off her body to us. And yes, it was very nice.

A few weeks later, Dr. Jack gave us news that would change our lives forever. He had bought a clinic in Southern Arizona, in a retirement community called Green Valley, south of Tucson.

CHAPTER 17

"Nooners" and then, Bankruptcy!

We were happy to leave California. It just didn't fit right. Like the pair of purple high heels that pinched my feet, the ones we bought in Bombay years ago. They still follow us around, move to move, waiting for my feet to shrink.

Renting another U-Haul, we loaded it, leaving behind some things that we hardly ever used, and replacing them with new things we had acquired. We headed out, east on I-10 after dark when the traffic was light.

We felt no remorse about leaving. Not right away, anyway. As Terry drove, my mind raced. Will this moving ever end? We weren't getting any younger. Terry was fifty-eight, and I was forty-eight. And what about this Green Valley? Was it like the tv series *Green Acres* with abundant fertile ground? We needed to get planted and grow some roots, homegrown roots.

Near midnight I turned on my Jeep's radio, and "Auld Lang Syne" was playing, telling me that the year 2006 had run out of time. The radio host said, "Happy New Year, everyone!"

I leaned toward Terry and whispered in his ear, "I love you," and kissed him on the cheek for good luck. Hours later, it was still dark when we passed through Tucson and headed south on I-19, the only highway in the U.S. with distance markers and exit signs posted in kilometers. Soon we took exit 69 into Green Valley.

When my husband saw the exit sign, he turned to me, looking briefly into my eyes as he squeezed my leg. He said, "Do you know what "69" means to some Americans? I said, "No?" He just smiled and said nothing.

The first thing we passed after the exit ramp was a Safeway supermarket, which was closed. I thought it odd even though it was New Year's Day. Then we turned left at a street light, and we passed a Circle K, also closed. In California, they were open 24 hours. Driving further down the dark street with no street lights, we found a Best Western Motel and checked in. Terry asked the motel clerk why it was so quiet around town, especially on the turning of the year?

He replied, "People around here go to bed early because they are retired." I wondered if we would fit in with a community of people who no longer worked for a living?

We got the room key, showered, then slipped into bed. I knocked three times on the wooden headboard for good luck. My husband heard me but said nothing, as we fell into one another slowly with deep passion. I thought to myself, "What a pleasant way to start a new year."

The following day we met Dr. Jack and Dianna at the house where they had prearranged for us to live. It was nice, but to my surprise it had a rock lawn and garden. So why was this town called Green Valley?

We unloaded the U-Haul for the fourth time. I told Terry to be careful with the TV, but my warning fell on deaf ears or perhaps foreshadowed a self-fulfilling prophecy on my part. He accidentally caught it on the side of the trailer, thereby smashing it to bits. I held back my urge to say something cruel and bit my lip since my fear of breaking it most likely played into the outcome. After all, it was a heavy set, and I should have known Terry would need to prove his strength to me by carrying it all by himself.

The next morning, we drove to the new clinic, which was called "The First Resort." It was only a few blocks from our house. It already had a large client base from the previous doctor, and several patients were waiting to get IVs. Our job was to prepare them, but he had to teach us how. Dr. Jack taught Terry the formulas, and then he taught me. But I was very nervous because if I screwed up, it could be fatal for the patient.

The nurse who administered the IVs was a lady named Brinda, and I had difficulty getting along with her. It was her way or no way. On occasion, she had could be very bossy, even when she was talking to Dr. Jack. Whenever she treated him this way, he would give her a cold stare and say nothing. Dr. Jack could be stern, but for the most part, he was easygoing.

Terry, however, seemed to get along with her without difficulty. Even so, he told me she reminded him of "Nurse Ratched," from the movie *One Flew Over the Cuckoo's Nest*, with Jack Nicholson. I had never seen the movie, so my husband's attempt to help me better understand fell short. Then, some weeks later, after replacing the TV we had broken together, we rented the movie. My husband was spot on; we were working with Nurse Ratched, a viciously officious, humorless, rigid person who took out her own frustrations on those around her.

But in spite of Nurse Ratched, all in all, we were having fun working at Dr. Jack's clinic. Business was good, and that meant we felt financially secure. I have to say, getting up at 8 A.M. proved a bit early for us, though. At the body shop we were used to arranging our work hours to suit ourselves. Some days, however, we would return home at noon, which was a bonus for both of us. We would walk past our bed, stop, look into each other's eyes with passion, and then Terry and I would undress and have what he called a "nooner." These brief occasional encounters did the trick. They were the pick-me-up passion that kept us going during difficult weeks.

A few months later, Dr. Jack changed the clinic's name, rebranding it "Back to Health," and our client base continued to grow. My husband and I got our Naturopathic Medical Assistant certificates, which expanded our duties to giving injections and starting IVs on patients.

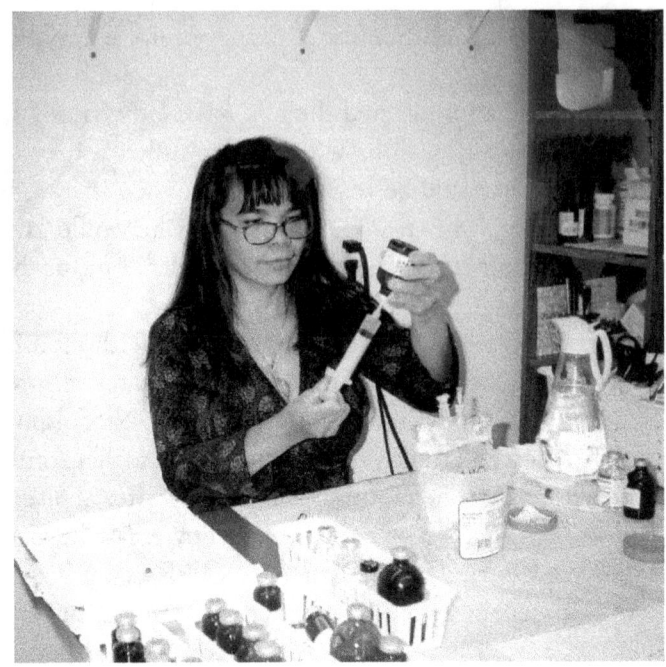

Above, we see Pedo working as a physician assistant (as was Terry) for Dr. Jack Hinze, a natural path practitioner in the States in Green Valley, AZ.

Most of our patients were a pleasure to be with, like Nancy Overton, a pop singer formerly with The Chordettes, an all-female quartet from the 1950s. One popular song which they recorded was "Lolly Pop." When it came to the part where they sang, "Lolly Pop, Lolly Pop, ooh, Lolly, Lolly Pop," etc., Nancy was the singer who made the 'POP!' sound in the recording. She stuck her forefinger into her mouth and showed us how she did it.

When she was touring with the group, she traveled with Dean Martin and Jerry Lewis, and she shared many stories about their escapades. A year later, Terry received a phone call from Nancy. She said in a very quiet and raspy voice, "Hello, Terry. I am on my deathbed, and my family is around me. I can't talk for long. I just wanted to thank you and Pedo for helping me while in Green Valley. It meant a great deal to me. Thank you. This made us both feel we were doing something important."

We treated another patient who turned out to be something of a crazy lady. She would come to see Dr. Jack and would seem to be perfectly normal at the moment. Then, out of the blue, she would get up, leave the office and drive off somewhere around Green Valley. Then she would pull over the car and stop in a panic and call the clinic. She demanded that Terry come and get her and bring her back. Dr. Jack had us administer what he called a placebo IV. Even though it was just like the other IVs, it was only a saline (water) solution. Dr. Jack assured her that these would help calm her down. Over time, they did seem to help her even though there was nothing special in them.

There was only one patient who made me particularly jealous. Terry and I were doing a breast thermal on this lady who only had one breast. Another doctor had removed the other one by mistake through a misdiagnosis of cancer before she came to our clinic. She had to be naked from the waist up to do the thermal examination.

After Terry took the picture, he would bring it up on his computer screen. As he was sitting facing the screen picture, the lady came up behind him and rested her one breast upon Terry's shoulder while they were both looking at the picture.

Terry appeared somewhat shocked by what she was doing, and he began to readjust himself in his seat. On the other hand, I knew she was teasing him, as she flirted with my husband while I was there in the room.

Finally, I'd had enough. I looked at her and said, "Okay. Back off! You've seen enough." I do admit, though, that she did have a nice breast for a solo.

We were still renting our house, even though I thought it was a waste of money. I wanted to get our own home because it now seemed we would be living in Green Valley for a long time. Terry tried to get a home loan, but the banks turned us down because of poor credit scores. Our travels to Asia had led to Terry maxing out his credit cards, thereby affecting his FICO credit score.

One afternoon Dianna overheard Terry on the phone, trying to get a mortgage. After he hung up, she said, "I didn't know you and Pedo wanted to buy a house. If you would like me to help out, I would be happy to buy one for you. All you have to do is pay me back in cash."

We were both dumbfounded by the trust and kindness that Dianna was willing to offer us.

Terry said, "What if we can't pay you back?"

She smiled and said, "The worst thing that could happen is I would just own another house."

Shortly after that, I spotted a house that was for sale. It was on a corner lot, and it had a big backyard with trees and plenty of space for my garden. Before setting up a showing with the realtor, Terry and I went and sat in the backyard patio. It felt perfect!

When the realtor came and let us in the front door, we instantly felt at home, blue shag carpet and all. After we moved in, we remodeled the whole interior by ourselves. It was 2011. I was fifty-three, and my husband was sixty-three.

Things seemed to be going great. A year or so later, Dr. Jack decided it was time to retire, so he sold Back to Health to another naturopath, he and Dianna built a house down in Patagonia, and worked part-time through phone consulting.

Our new boss's name was Dr. Mayfield. He was a tall man with white hair, and he had a keen sense of humor. His girlfriend, a younger woman named Barb, was an Austrian, and she spoke with a heavy accent. I had difficulty understanding her, but she was a beauty. Terry thought she was very sexy. We had fun working with Barb, and Dr. Mayfield.

Unfortunately, however, the new owners turned out to be poor business managers. Later that year, they gathered the staff and told everyone they had filed for bankruptcy. It came as a shock to all of us when Dr. Mayfield told us we would not be getting a paycheck. Instead, he said, "Take whatever you want from the clinic and do it before 5:00 P.M. because that's when the bank is going to change the locks.

There was a flurry of activity from the staff as they went around the clinic, grabbing whatever they felt might be of value. Terry took an excellent weight scale and a potted tree which flourished under my care. But I wondered if the same would be true for us. We now had no job, a house to pay for, along with my Jeep, which was ready for a brake job. I looked at Terry as we walked out the clinic door just before 5:00 P.M. that day. We were scared. There was fear in our eyes.

CHAPTER 18

TRAPPING THE MEMORIES FROM MY PAST

It was now time to find work. Terry applied at Walmart, but he didn't get any response. When he told me he had a college degree, part of me felt as though he was fooling around with me. I believed, for sure, Terry would have made a marvelous greeter. After failing to get a job at Walmart, he went to Ace Hardware. They told him he could help by mixing paint for customers, but for some reason, it didn't feel right to him.

As for myself, I had my Malaysian diploma from Anita Hair and Beauty Salon in Kuching. I graduated from there in October of 1998. After a couple of attempts, I discovered this degree did not qualify me for work in the U.S.A. Instead, I would have to take all the classes over again at the community college in Tucson. And there, I would be competing with students who were young enough to be my children. It seemed highly ironic to me that after my years of experience in Malaysia, I could have taught them, which of course was not an option for me. And then, after working for years with my husband, the bottom line was to find a job that we could do together, bonded at the hips, taking on life together.

It was a Friday night, and we were sitting in front of the TV trying to find a program worth watching after downgrading our monthly internet package to a lower price. I was sewing, and Terry was flipping through the channels. My grandfather once said, "Pedo, remember this: Most things you need in life can be found right under your nose. All you need to do is to slow down and take a look."

I turned to Terry, smiled, and in a moment of silent agreement, we spoke at the same time and said, "Why don't we start a body shop?" On Monday morning, we put an ad in *The Green Valley News*. "Retired body shop man looking for work in his shop." The only problem was we didn't have a shop. It was the fall of 2009.

We never expected much of a response after the ad came out. Happily, though, with blind foresight, we had brought with us the hand tools and spray guns from Nebraska. Using Terry's Home Depot credit card, we bought an air compressor, which we put into our garage. Soon the first customer with a car needing work arrived, so we revved up the compressor for a paint job. But the noise and fumes bothered our neighbors, and the fumes also got into our house. We had to find another shop quickly. Time and money were at stake, so we needed to move fast. Luckily, we located a small warehouse in Amado, a small town about eleven miles from where we lived. After a short drive, we set up our new body shop in Amado a day later.

An idea popped into my head, and I said to Terry, "We need to get some T-shirts with our logo printed on them so that we look like professionals." Terry thought it was a good idea, so, I picked out the colors purple and pink; he winced at the combination but said, "Let's go with your colors," and we had "Iwanski Body Shop" silk screened on the back.

The only problem with the shirts was my name, Pedo. One day, one of our Spanish-speaking customers, while paying his bill, asked me politely, "Pedo, is that really your name?"

I smiled and said, "Yes, it is."

The man looked down at his shoes, and with some reluctance said, "Well, you know, in our language, the word "pedo" means fart." Then, he looked up at me and smiled. I chuckled, smiled, and then told him, "In my native language, the word 'pedo' means 'I see the moon.'"

Later, Terry laughed and told me he thought "fart" was an appropriate name for me. Even so, my name would prove to be only a minor problem in the future.

We didn't expect the business to grow as fast as it did. At times we had so many jobs we were overwhelmed. And some of our tools were outdated or worn out from so much use. After only a few months, we had to buy a bigger compressor to keep up with so many customers. We worked hard, sometimes even into the night.

For the most part, our business grew because we catered mainly to senior citizens, and we didn't charge outrageous prices knowing they were all on fixed incomes. Plus, we did the 'old school' style of bodywork, which they remembered from earlier days, instead of just replacing parts, which often made the job more expensive.

However, the main problem, which caused the most trouble, was getting supplies from Tucson. Often, we had to get up early and drive into Tucson for supplies, which ended up killing half the day. So, we ended up contracting with two parts suppliers in Tucson that would deliver. We hired retired people as 'go-getters' for paint supplies, which turned out great, a win-win situation for all.

The shop took on a life of its own. By 2015 we had our house paid for because I told Terry from the start that we needed to focus on that, and he agreed with me. We had a new front door installed to celebrate, and then we decided to celebrate by taking a trip and treating ourselves to first class tickets back to Malaysia to see my family. At first, I was shocked by the cost of first-class tickets compared to economy. But then I thought it was time to spoil my husband a bit; he's such a hard worker and a good lover. So, I said nothing.

Before leaving, I had much to prepare and pack. And in the end, I did all of it since Terry didn't even offer to help because he knew I had to do it my way. Also, I like to bring presents back for my family, and anything made in the USA is a big deal to them. So, I decided to get shoes, probably because I didn't have any when I was a kid. I bought them for my whole family, including my abusive uncle. When Terry found out I did this, he said, "Why the hell did you buy shoes for him?" I couldn't come up with an answer.

Then there were my clothes to pack, three bags full, an outfit change for every day, plus some shoes. I did, however, leave my purple heels at home, finally conceding they would never fit me again.

Before packing Terry's clothes in a small carry on, I flashed back in time to the day I met him in Bangkok after we were married. Then, it was me who stepped off the plane with a tiny brown paper sack with one pair of silk panties in it. I have certainly come a long way since then, and I am so proud of myself.

The bags turned out to be very heavy and, as Terry dragged them along through the airport, I still remember his complaints about packing too much stuff. When we got to the check-in counter, Terry looked at me with a frown on his face as the lady weighed each bag separately. She looked at us and said, "Well, the total comes to two-hundred dollars. My husband looked at me and said nothing. I bet he was thinking, "For that kind of money, we could have bought the family and neighbors complete outfits, seeing how the exchange rate for US dollars was four Ringgits to one."

After a short flight from Tucson to Los Angeles LAX, the baggage carriers, lucky for us, transferred our luggage to Singapore Airlines. LAX is a huge airport, and it would have been horrible if we had had to drag all of it to the next gate. When we got to our gate, we started to experience the perks of flying first class. We were able to board first, spoiled from the get-go. And we liked it.

Once we were on the plane, a stewardess took us to our respective seating areas, which she could turn into a bed if we so desired. She would also re-make the bed at our request. But my seat was not an armchair close to my husband. So, I would sometimes go over to his bed and snuggle close to him.

The food, too, was outstanding, and Terry had as much beer as he wanted, which he was glad to accept from the beautiful Asian stewardesses, who kept him well supplied. We also had a separate and unique lounge we could go to on stopovers. We had the best of everything. Our last stop was in Singapore, where we had to board Malaysia Airlines to Kuching. We were armchair close in First Class this time, but it was a short flight.

We landed, and the stewardess opened the cabin door. Upon reaching the door, I breathed in the thick, moist air I remembered from childhood. As I took a deep breath, it felt as though I was filling up my lungs with home. After renting a car, Terry loaded our luggage into the trunk and back seat. I took the front passenger seat, on the vehicle's front left side. Terry would be driving the car sitting in the front right seat, which was the opposite of what he was used to doing. He was also using an international license he had qualified for back in the states. I still had my Malaysian driver's license but preferred to let him do the driving. I was a bit nervous, so I found myself carefully observing him because driving on the left was new to him. He looked at me and said, "Don't worry. I'm getting the hang of this."

That night we stayed at the Grand Margherita Hotel in downtown Kuching. It was an upscale building and yet inexpensive. My husband liked it because he could see the Sarawak River from our fifth-floor window. And he was delighted to see a McDonald's down below across the street. Sometimes he has a difficult time appreciating good Asian food.

I was so excited about being home that I had difficulty sleeping that night. We awoke early and went down to the lobby to enjoy a lavish complimentary breakfast, half Asian and half British cuisine.

I first wanted to go to Kampung Gerung, my jungle home. The streets were busy in the city, making us both tense with all the heavy traffic. Kuching was growing so fast that I could barely recognize it anymore. Finally, we made it to a roundabout I remembered on the edge of town. I then saw a sign that said, "Serian," a town I knew well, with an arrow pointing the way to go, so I told Terry to follow the sign. I sighed and tried to relax. But we were coming close to some places that triggered unwanted memories from my past.

The traffic here was light, so we had time to enjoy the scenery. Soon the countryside turned to a lush green with gray, rocky peaks off in the distance wreathed with mist. We passed several old wooden shacks that served as bus stops along the way, with trails that led off into the jungle. Then we passed a large cemetery with many ornate white monuments. The thought of burning my beloved grandfather's body in the deep jungle, with only the green overgrowth of plants to cover him, brought me a tinge of shame. I had desperately wanted to see him properly sent to the next world, but when I found out he had died, my boss wouldn't let me off from work, no matter how much I pleaded with him.

Now, I thought back to how it could have been different. If I had been there, perhaps I would have been able at least to provide a headstone in his memory. But maybe it was best for him to remain in the jungle.

I looked up from my thoughts and saw the sign for Kampung Gerung. I then became aware that my eyes had begun to fill with tears. As I reached up and wiped them dry, Terry let me have my private space and said nothing. The road narrowed as we turned, soon to become less than a single lane, made of rough asphalt and rock. I was getting close to home. Terry parked the car, and we walked across a small wooden bridge to get to my Kampung. The village had grown over the years. Many more huts were crowded together as if for safety from the jungle. It was much changed from what I remembered. People had built some of these newer huts with concrete, others out of wood, lumber from the city-—a significant upgrade from my father's and uncle's huts made from bamboo and sago leaves. Skinny dogs were barking on either side of us while clucking chickens pecked at the ground beneath their feet.

Only one or two people remembered me as we walked through the village. I was bothered by this a bit, but then again, I was only twelve years old when I left. I found an old lady and asked her if she knew where my Uncle Rupa lived. To my surprise, she said, "Yes.'" and led us around the labyrinth of walkways.

She stopped in front of a concrete hut, the door of which was wide open because of the heat of the day. I thanked her and slipped her a few dollars. She smiled at me and walked away. We knocked on the door then stepped in, finding my uncle half-naked and asleep on the bare concrete floor. He was, however, not how I remembered him. I knelt on the floor and attempted to wake him.

"Uncle," I said, "please wake up." He sat up, startled. We looked at one another, and in an instant, I recognized him. "It's me," I said, "Pedo." He blinked twice, then said, "Hello Pedo," in our jungle language. "You have grown." I then introduced him to Terry, and they both smiled and nodded at one another.

I believe his anger toward me had long ago disappeared into the deep, brown wrinkles that had formed upon his face and forehead. I then noticed his feet, which were now twisted and deformed because he never wore shoes. I quickly pulled out the new pair of shoes I had purchased for him back in the states, along with some money Terry gave me.

We didn't talk much, but that wasn't entirely a surprise. When I had last seen him, he didn't know I was getting ready to run away. And since then, we had, I was sure, lived very different lives. So, I was resigned to the fact that we didn't have much to say to each other.

I felt sorry for my uncle, even though he had always treated me badly, even to the point of physical cruelty. But seeing him now, he looked terribly old, and broken. And he was not much longer for this life, because he died just a few months later. "Dust to dust, ashes to ashes," just as my grandfather had died and become part of the jungle. I was, however, happy that I had a chance to see him before he was gone.

After saying goodbye to my uncle, I asked someone where the "mute girl" in the village lived. Everybody knew her, so it was easy to find her. She lived with her mother. Oddly enough, everyone always referred to her as "the mute girl," as if she didn't even have a name. Her real name was Noney, and she was a childhood friend. She was born mute and didn't have any education. It sure would have been different for her if she had been born in America. We were good friends, and I remembered how she would often try to speak, but nothing ever came out of her mouth except for her effort and frustration but after a while I was able to understand her hand movements.

I gave her the new clothes and offered her some money as I had done with my uncle. She was overjoyed as she tried on her new clothes, on the spot. Terry stepped aside and looked at her with a big smile on his face. He pointed at her, and with gestures, he seemed to be trying to say, "You look beautiful!"

Next, we took off on foot for the long walk to my father's house. He had built his house on a hill, and he only had one neighbor. Someone had put in thirty concrete steps which led up to his home. There was an abandoned bus stop at the bottom of the hill, where the steps began. No one had used it for years. The last one to live in the two-room house was my mother. My father had constructed the home long ago, but now the walls looked tired, and someone had even replaced the sago leaves on top with a tin roof. Furthermore, mice and the natural impact of nature had taken over the inside of the house.

One of my dreams was to see all my brothers and sisters at the old house on the hill. I also wanted to invite some friends. So, I asked my younger sister Poni to contact everyone and let them know about the party. It was, however, a difficult job because most of them didn't have phones or cars.

My sister and I climbed thirty steps back up to my father's house and cleaned the inside in preparation for the event. While we did this, Terry decided to walk around the village looking for some cold beer for the party and himself, which he found.

On the day of the party, we brought in food and drinks, with lots of beer and whiskey. Of course, in the back of my mind, I knew once the word got out, the whole village would show up, and they did. It was a good time, and the party went on into the night. Terry and one of the villagers he met decided to build a bonfire.

It was a wonderful time. I enjoyed being with my family and friends. By late night, people began to drift home, many of them staggering as best as they could, having consumed far too much alcohol. And because there is no lower age limit on drinking in Kampong Gerung, some people were kids as young as twelve years old. When Terry and I finished up and got ready to go back to our hotel, I insisted that I do the driving, which I did.

The following day we went back to the village and hired a local contractor to fix up my father's house, hoping that one of my brothers would choose to live there. We would also have a concrete living space with an inside toilet, water, and electricity. And then we bought the land next door, and had the ground leveled out a plot where we might build a new house, and graded a road leading up to it, just in case Terry and I ever decided to construct our own jungle home in the future. But for the short term, we bought a small three-bedroom apartment in Kuching before we left, which gave us a place to stay instead of the Grand Margherita.

We once again had enjoyed a good time in Malaysia. We always do, for the most part. But it was time for us to go home and get back to work. The contractors assured us they would send us photos of their progress at my father's house and on the land where we might build our little home-away-from-home one day, which they did. But to this day, my father's house still stands vacant, and the land we purchased next to it remains overgrown by 'my' jungle. I offered my brothers and sisters to live in it for free, but they wanted to stay in Kuching. I offered it to my father, too, but he scared to stay in it alone.

The last few days in Kuching, Terry and I walked around town looking for places I could remember. But, of course, as is often the case, most of these places had changed significantly, or they were gone. But one still stood as it was when I was young. It was the theater in front of which my friend Somoy and I used to stand, and one day got into a fight with a prostitute who believed this was her turf. I smiled to myself because that was a battle that we had won.

But my next footstep triggered the memory of where I had met Hee Ping, the man who broke my heart by leaving me after getting me pregnant. And, of course, Hee Ping's betrayal was the first straw that created in me a basic mistrust of men. Thinking about him made me feel grateful for Terry and our daughter Aling. As we walked along, I squeezed his hand with tenderness.

We stopped and ate at an outdoor restaurant, which reminded me of where I worked when my grandfather died, where my boss wouldn't let me go home for the funeral. As I swallowed the food, a bitter taste began to form in my mouth.

At last, we found Kuching Plaza, where I worked as a hairstylist and where I first met Terry so many years ago. To my surprise, the shop was vacant, and the whole building was standing alone and empty. It made me sad to see that part of my past gone. But I reached down and grabbed hold of Terry's hand. I was not standing alone.

We walked back to the Grand Margherita Hotel, where we were still staying because our apartment had not yet been cleaned, painted, or furnished. Nevertheless, it was time for us to head back to our home in the states. So, we packed our belongings, and checked out. Before leaving, we left a healthy tip for both the maid and the bellboy. I had to show Terry the way back to the airport, and once there, we turned in our car with the steering wheel on the right side and paid our bill. Then we boarded the short armchair flight to back Singapore, and the stewardess closed the cabin door, trapping forever the memories from my past.

CHAPTER 19

THE DEMONS FROM MY PAST DISAPPEARED.

I had many thoughts about my family during the flights home. I felt sorry for them; they got by with next to nothing. The worst off was my younger sister Poni, who lived with her family in a wooden shack built on the side of a hill. It had a door, but no glass in any of the windows.

And here I was, living in America and making good money. I felt I should be giving them more than just shoes and a few dollars here and there. My mind was tortured, as I was torn between guilt and greed. Where was my middle ground? And then, what did my family expect from me? I knew I had to think of myself first. I took all the risks when I met my husband in the salon years ago. It was my job to take care of him and our daughter. I then decided to help them after fulfilling our needs first, which we would do.

Then, as I sat there thinking, our smooth flight thus far turned into turbulence and the seat belt sign came on. I was scared and so I squeezed in with Terry; there was more than enough room. A stewardess saw me do this but said nothing as she sat down and strapped herself into her jump-seat.

We landed several hours later with little luggage to carry through LAX. Everything we had was in either a small carry-on suitcase with wheels or a small day pack we could carry on our backs, which was a great relief to my husband. The flight back to Tucson was short, and when we landed and the stewardess opened the cabin door it was stifling for me, as the hot, dry air from outside filled the cabin inside, making it hard for me to breathe.

We made our way to the long-term parking area where we had left my Jeep. As we walked up to her, I saw the paint had faded in the hot Arizona sun. She was losing her makeup, and when I told my husband it was time for a new paint job, he said, "No, Pedo. It wouldn't be worth the time or effort." So, I said, "Well then, you're going to have to buy me a new car!" And that caused him to fall silent.

When we got home, Terry had dozens of messages on his phone even though he had left a recording, which said: "Please don't leave a message. We will be on vacation for thirty days." The machine would not take any more.

We were blessed with business and worked hard day after day to the point of exhaustion. But we were happy to be on our own, free to again pick our working hours. One of the services we offered clients was free pick-up and delivery. One day, while looking for a street address, I spotted the car of my dreams, which had a For Sale sign in the front window; it was a bright yellow Audi TT Convertible. I looked and Terry and said, "I want that car!" He bought it for me on the spot.

When it came time to get the license plates for my new car, I wanted them personalized with the two words, "Sugar Daddy." We went to the DMV, filled out the form, paid for these special plates, and one week later, I had my plates. As my husband put them on the back of my car, I looked at him with a big smile and said, "I am one proud girl!"

It was time to sell my Jeep, which had served me well. But by now, she was dripping oil on our driveway. Terry looked at me and said, "Sorry, Pedo, but it's time to let her go." We parked her in front of our house. This time with the same For Sale sign from my new care in her window. We sold her in one day, and her new owner took her across the border to Mexico. And we'd sold her at a profit! I was happy and waved goodbye to her, with a tear in my eye, thanking her for her years of good service.

But now, we were in somewhat of a bind. We were not going to use my new little yellow Audi for hauling parts. She was in pristine shape, and I certainly didn't want her all torn up doing so. According to my husband, she, like me, was now high maintenance. I didn't understand what he meant. I looked at him and said, "What do you mean? I'm not a car."

But good luck with cars seemed to come our way. Our bookkeeper, Rose, drove a newer Nissan Murano SL, a very high-end car. Someone came along one day and hit her vehicle on the side, making it undrivable. She called Terry and asked him if he wanted to buy it, for a low price, since she had collected a reasonable payment from her insurance company. Terry said, "yes," bought it, and then fixed it up. And, of course, the Nissan Murano SL became my new car.

When it came time for new license plates, I decided to personalize them again. We went to the DMV, filled out the paperwork, and paid the fee. When asked by the clerk what I had written, I said, "AKU Pedo," which means I am Pedo, in my national language Bahasa, and that was it.

One week later, the head office of the Arizona Department of Transportation sent us a letter telling us that what I had written was inappropriate language for a license plate. Terry looked at me and smiled. Again, the meaning of pedo got in the way. They assumed I wanted to have 'I am a fart' on my new license plate. "Well," he said, "I'll take care of this." He called the DMV and asked them if they were having trouble with the word "Pedo?" They said, "Yes, you cannot use that word." Terry replied, "Well, that's her real name. And he sent them a copy of my driver's license. A week or so later, I got my new plates.

My husband also bought a car for himself, a wretched little Mini Cooper S, which needed repairs. After doing the necessary repairs, he put normal plates on his car, which now sits parked outside in our driveway while my girls--my two cars--rest, pampered in our garage behind a locked iron gate, waiting for me to wake them up.

The years have passed, one after the other, as the wrinkles on my husband's face have done the same. But I still find him attractive. Lucky for me, I have remained wrinkleless so far, mainly because most Asians remain clear-skinned until advanced age, and then it happens quickly. Such was the case for my mom and dad.

We tried to take a trip every year in July when the weather in Arizona gets unbearably hot. Once we went to Hongkong, which we found boring for the most part. We went to Bangkok twice, which proved to be more exciting, as it was when we first met after our marriage, along with a three-month separation in between. Then came Indonesia, where we ventured deep into the jungle on dirt roads using a hired driver. It was unfortunate when Terry got carsick while traveling upon the rough, trail-like roads.

Closer to home, we traveled to Mexico, where one time, I was detained at the border while trying to get back to the states in Nogales. I had foolishly forgotten my Malaysian passport, and just as had happened to us at LAX in Los Angeles, the immigration officers wouldn't let my husband go along with me for questioning. I was terrified of being prevented from crossing the U.S. border, only forty-four miles from my home. Fortunately, when they saw my anxiety reaching a total panic level, they allowed Terry to come into the conversation to help resolve my dilemma.

My favorite close-to-home escapade turned out to be a trip to Caesar's Palace in Las Vegas. The flight from Tucson is not only inexpensive but short. I like to gamble, even though my husband does not. He is content to sit with a beer in hand and watch the girls go by, which is not a problem since I know that I am his natural choice of eye-candy, I am always ready to satisfy his needs, and we both know it.

I play slot machines, and sometimes I return to my husband with a sizeable amount of money. It excites me when the bell rings in my favor followed by a cascade of coins, and I like the challenge of it. Later that night, I find we can often celebrate my winnings a second time, this time in bed.

One day, as we walked around the casino, Terry spotted a 21 table with an attractive female Asian dealer sitting there alone. My husband looked at me and said, "Why don't you give it a try? You're fast at cards." With some prodding, I sat down opposite the Asian girl and started to play. To my surprise, I started winning, not just once, but again and again. *This is fun*, I thought to myself. And soon, I was up a few hundred dollars, more than I had ever made with the slot machines. Then, the dealer got up out of the blue, and an attractive white lady replaced her.

Before I knew it, my winnings began to dwindle, and soon this new young white girl had won back my entire stash to her side of the table. Then I realized the Asian girl was helping me to win. I was so embarrassed. What had just happened to me? I turned away from the table and went back to playing the slots. Terry returned to his beer and watched the other ladies, but soon, he became bored waiting for me. When he gambles, he never wins. But when we got back to our room later that night, we were both winners with each other in bed.

After a few days in Vegas, we grew tired but sadly not wealthy. That elusive goal brings many to the thrill of gambling, but few bask in the joy of becoming winners. Our pay-off was spending time together, far away from the toxic fumes of the shop. We went to the airport by taxi, and Terry tipped the driver as he has done so many times before. Unlike what he had done for me so many years before, I realized he just didn't know any better. I have forgiven him. Anyway, he has always been generous to my family and me over the years. And I love him for it.

We arrived in Tucson late that night. But it was such a short trip that by the time the stewardess had served everyone a drink, she had to turn around and come back to pick them up. It didn't seem worth the effort. As our small plane circled the airport, we could see the lights of the city twinkle against its black backdrop.

It was a smooth landing as the plane's wheels touched down on the runway and soon pulled into its arrival gate, and we deboarded with our small carry-ons. The airport was eerily empty this late at night, which was okay with me. As Terry and I slowly made our way over to long-term parking where we left his Mini, I turned to him and said, "I hope it starts," thinking about the time mine didn't. Luckily, it did.

And off we went on the short drive back to Green Valley and our home. The traffic was light at this time of night, so we were there before we knew it. We parked his car in front of the gated garage where my vehicles were waiting for me. As usual, Terry went first, unlocked the dark house, then turned to me and said, "We're here, sweetheart."

Since childhood, I've always been scared of the dark. Where things went bump in the blackness of the jungle without being seen. As Terry unlocked the door and flipped on the lights, I stood in fear. Then, the demons from my past disappeared. We were home.

CHAPTER 20

Work is work, and Play is play.

After the noise of Vegas, we took a few days off to enjoy our home and the peace and quiet of Green Valley. And it gave me time to pull my yellow car out of the garage and wash her after having been dusted with a fine coat of desert sand.

It was a warm afternoon, so I put the top down and headed towards the nearby town of Sahuarita. I needed some time to be just . . . me. The wind in my hair tickled some memories alive, and I thought about how much trouble I had getting my driver's license in Kuching when I was but twenty. Even though I did not have a car, I thought it would be a good idea to get one. No one in my family had ever had a driver's license. I would be the first.

It took me four tries to pass the written test presented in Bahasa and English. But my reading skills in English were less than stellar at the time, because I had left the Kampong school early, thanks to my uncle's abuse. When I finally passed, next came the dreaded driving test. The license bureau supplied the car, a stick-shift, not an automatic! And I had never driven a car before, no less a stick! I was petrified. So many things to remember and coordinate! The male test supervisor, who was seated to my left, had his own set of foot controls but no steering wheel. He made me so nervous. Then, before I knew what was happening, we were off with a grinding of gears and a jerk of the car, headed toward downtown Kuching. When I glanced at him, he seemed calm and relaxed. His nerves were of steel; mine, however, felt like noodles. And yet, I surprised myself, doing well on the test and making just a few minor blunders. So, I got my license and have kept it current over the years with some effort on my part.

I did better when I got my U.S. driver's license in Lincoln, Nebraska. The written test offered me several more choices of languages. I chose English. This time, it took me only three tries to pass it, one better than in Kuching. And the driving test was a piece of cake because I was allowed to drive my pearl-white Nissan Pulsar with an automatic shift. I made only one mistake. After taking a right turn, I should have stayed in the far-right lane instead of pulling over to the left lane. I turned to my male supervisor and gave him my biggest smile, and he let it go. I was so proud of myself.

Over the years, I have only gotten one ticket, a violation for running a red-light in Green Valley. The officer was mistaken, so my husband took it to court. When Terry asked if he could speak in my defense, the judge asked him I could speak English.

When he said, "Yes. But she might not understand some of the words," the judge said, "She can speak for herself."

So, I had to defend myself, and the judge ruled against me, which meant we ended up paying a two hundred fifty-dollar fine.

When, back in the present, I pulled my car back into the garage, my mind stopped focusing on the past, and reality set in. I was happy to be home again with my husband. That evening after dark, we sat out back on our patio, enjoying a drink. We were facing south and could see dark clouds in flashes of lighting.

Terry said, "I bet Amado is getting hammered."

We finished our drinks, went inside, and slid into bed. We watched the old black and white movie, *The Night of the Hunter,* starring Robert Mitchum, as a corrupt, sociopathic minister who was also a serial killer, and Shelley Winters, one of his victims, which we both enjoyed.

In the morning, we got up without the aid of an alarm clock. Our inner ones were well set for 9:00 A.M. We had our coffee and headed for our shop in Amado. It was Labor Day, September 3, 2018.

When we arrived at our shop, we found the chain-link gate and the rest of the fence which surrounded Amado feed and RV storage.

Our body shop was in the same building. There was enough standing water that one needed hip waders to get to the office. Terry waded in only with his jeans while I stayed in the car. He waded into the building over top of the knocked-down front doors with shattered glass. He then walked over the hundreds of semi-floating feed sacks strewn about to get to our shop door.

Once inside, Terry told me he was petrified by what he discovered. As he climbed around the debris, he kept running into one rattlesnake after another. When he moved the refrigerator to one side, a large rattler, seemingly asleep, sat just above the cold water. After dislodging a large steel shelf, he found several smaller rattlers looking for their mother.

Making his way to our shop door, Terry found everything destroyed; our compressors and all of our tools. Even our large paint inventory had been flooded away, with the labels on most of the cans washed off by dirty water. The whole place stank of horse manure from the several surrounding ranches—and the water had destroyed almost everything we had in our shop.

But Amado feed and storage had it worse. The raging wall of water had swept over ninety-six motor homes, destroying them as they floated towards the Sopri creek. The town folk would call this a hundred-year flood. But we were lucky that we hadn't been there in the early morning when the flood came through. Had we been, we would have surely drowned.

It took us over a month to clean up our shop. We also helped Amado Feed, where all those bags had come from. All in all, it was hard, dirty, stinky, and mucky work! The dried mud turned into a fine dust that seeped into the concrete floors and took months for us to completely sweep away. Sadly, Amado Feed and Iwanski Body Shop had no flood insurance. Who would have imagined a hundred-year flood in the middle of the desert?

Over the previous few months, our daughter Aling and I had spoken on the phone more often, and I could tell by her voice that things were not going well for her and her husband, Matthew.

She told me she was being left alone by Matthew often at night with the kids, and she was afraid for herself and her children, a two-month-old baby named Matt, a five-year-old toddler named Jaydyn, and a ten-year-old adolescent named Minnie Belle.

And to make the situation even more severe, her husband physically abused Aling and even the kids. Aling decided it was time to divorce him. I knew that Aling needed help, but she was headstrong and too proud to ask for help like me. So, without being asked, Terry and I offered to move her and her children to Green Valley to be near us. We hired a mover to help her move her stuff here, and she would drive herself and her children here in her car.

Late on Christmas Eve, 2018, Aling and her children knocked on our door full of smiles and hugs. Her oldest child, Minnie Belle, was sixteen and proved to be my husband's intellectual challenge. Jaydin was thirteen with dark, searching eyes and long tendrils of black hair, an artist. And her youngest was Matt, twelve years old, who would become Grampa's gym buddy and someone who would patiently listen to his many stories. After celebrating Christmas, they slept at our house and stayed with us. Our house was now a busy place.

A few weeks later, Aling found a job as a physician's assistant at a dermatology clinic in Tucson. Finding a place to live was a harder, but finally she found a lovely apartment not far from where we lived, and she enrolled her children in nearby schools.

When Aling and her kids joined us in Arizona, weekends changed for us. She and her kids enjoyed having family around. However, once winter edged into spring, Aling and the kids suffered the way all newcomers from more temperate climates did in the sweltering, dry Arizona climate.

One of our customers told me that living in Arizona will turn your blood into tomato soup, so you go from Arizona to a colder clime, you get cold quickly, unlike in Chicago, where it can get really hot in the summer, but in the spring and fall, it gets cooler, and in the winter it's cold, not just at night, but during the daytime too.

It took some time for Aling and the kids to adjust to the warmer climate and temperatures, but not too long. Arizona has a way of spoiling people when it comes to the weather. So soon, Aling and the kids learned to do things outside, even in the Arizona winter.

We often cooked Asian dishes out on our patio, even in the summer. Having two cooks was better than just one. Terry, however, had never fully adapted his palate to Malaysian cuisine, so we would cook special meals for him. And for that, Terry appreciated our efforts.

Business continued to grow at our shop, at a fast pace. We even hired another retired body man part-time. On the other hand, though, it seemed that as time went on the more I learned about the business, the less Terry worked. At times, I would get bossy with him, arguing that he was not doing his fair share of the work. But when the day was over, on our drive home, our love for one another would overcome whatever complaints I may have made during work, and I would feel tender toward Terry as I always did, and say, "Work is work. And play is play." I would smile at him and tell him, "We make a good team." And it is true. We are a good team, both at home and at work. I love Terry, and he loves me.

CHAPTER 21

Tangled Tight by Love

The weather was getting hot, too warm for work. After all, it was July, and the snowbirds had already flocked back to their original northern nests. They are the staples of our automotive body business; bless them. I thought of my own distant nest, halfway around the world.

It was 2019, and both Terry's and my feet itched to travel back to Malaysia. The last time we were there, it became painfully clear to me that Kuching was forever changing and was now a progressive city compared to when I was a youth. Many of the places I remembered had changed or had been replaced by other buildings or businesses. But my jungle birthplace of Kampong Garung had changed little, except that some of the villagers were now getting electricity. The few who had it referred to it as "The Wire."

When I told Aling we were planning another trip back home she told me she wanted to take the children and go with us to show them their roots. We set a date for our departure and bought two first-class tickets. Aling had to get her children passports and take time off from her job, and time was running short. After a few weeks went by, Terry and I assumed that we would be traveling by ourselves. Aling and her children would have to miss this adventure.

Then one pleasant evening, Terry and I were eating supper on the patio when Aling came through the side gate. Normally, she would walk through the front door and into the house, using her own key. She said, "Hi, mom and dad," and then gave us both a kiss on the cheek. Then with a smile as mischievous as the grin of the

Cheshire Cat in *Alice in Wonderland*, she said, "I have a surprise for you both!"

The first thing out of Terry's mouth (and my mind) was, "You're pregnant! Is that the surprise?" A surprised look crossed her face, and she said in a no-nonsense voice, "No. That will never happen again." And I believed her. Like me, she is a strong-willed woman.

Aling then said, "My surprise is I have everything arranged to take my family to Malaysia with you and dad, and I was able to buy the tickets on my own. But we will get there one week later because of my work schedule."

I got up and went into the house, picked up my purse, came back outside, and handed Aling a one-hundred-dollar Ringgit Note, which I carried for good luck. I gave it to her and said, "Here, use this for cab fare to get you and the kids to the Grand Margherita Hotel. We always stay there for a few days because I like it, and they serve a great breakfast buffet."

Even though we had bought a small three-bedroom apartment years ago, staying at the Margherita had become a habit. So, we once again did the same for the first two days. And the hotel staff remembered us, probably because of my husband's generous tipping.

So, Terry and I flew on our schedule, leaving the body shop in the care of our part-time guy. It was a long flight from Arizona, but we were, like our last trip, comfortably seated in the luxury of first class. I was, however, worried about our daughter and her children on their trip, the upcoming week, cramped in the economy seating. I felt a tad guilty, then thought back to the trips Terry and I made while cramped in economy seats. I was lucky now to be seated where we were, in First Class, but we had earned it. Besides, I thought, Aling's kids were young, and even Aling herself was still relatively young. So they would be fine in economy, though tired and stiff when they arrived.

A week after we arrived in Kuching, I was not surprised when, as Aling and her children arrived late in the day, they were all dog-tired from their long flight. After many hugs, they went to their room.

The following day everyone slept in late, missing the breakfast buffet, so Terry took Matt across the street to McDonald's, and the girls and I went to a chicken rice cafe around the corner.

After eating, we met in the hotel lobby, and Terry said, "Well, it's time to go and rent a car." I stopped Terry and said, "No, wait just a minute. I have a surprise for you." I looked at my husband with my own Cheshire Cat smile, and said, "Come with me." And we went outside and then walked out into the parking lot.

Without his knowledge, I had called my sister, Juliana, while we were still in Green Valley. One good thing she and I had was we could have a conversation in our language without my husband knowing what was said. I had decided to buy him a car with Juliana's help. She arranged to deliver it to the hotel and left the keys at the front desk, and I had retrieved them earlier. When we got to the parking lot, Terry was surprised and delighted when I said, "Here, sweetheart, this is a car I bought for you with Juliana's help.

The kids came down, and we all piled into our new car and headed for our apartment. The gray Kia Canto had the steering wheel on the right side instead of the left, but I was already used to driving here, so I got into the driver's seat and drove, which was easy since it was an automatic. Getting there was not a problem because I knew the way. But things, however, had changed quite a bit since we had last stayed there. It used to be a quiet place within walking distance of a small grocery store where Terry had befriended the owner, a pleasant Chinese man named Alex.

But our peaceful and quiet apartment now had a whole new feeling and atmosphere because of one new tenant, a young Chinese man who had just been released from prison. I shuddered when a neighbor told me the judge had sentenced him for the attempted murder of his mother with a knife.

This strange man played annoying "thump, thump" music all night long with no regard for anyone else in our apartment building. And it seemed to be the same song, over and over again. It was impossible to get any sleep, so we asked the other tenants if anyone had ever confronted him. They said, "No," with fear in their eyes, because they were as scared of him as we were. I pitied the people who lived next door to him. At least our apartment was located two floors below his.

Lucky for us, some months earlier, we had put down a deposit on a new three-bedroom condominium in a Kuching gated community as a possible retirement home. The following day we drove there, first thing, and paid it off in full. But we still had to have air conditioners installed and buy new furniture. Unfortunately, this meant we were forced to stay a few more days in our tiny apartment with our unruly and scary neighbor two floors above. Aling and her children were afraid to sleep in their bedrooms because of the stories about this possibly dangerous and crazy new neighbor.

They decided to drag their mattresses out of their bedrooms and arrange them on the living room floor. I smiled as the children slept like puppies: all snuggled beside their mother, snug and safe.

My daughter and I had fun buying all new furniture, lighting fixtures, and kitchen appliances for our new house, While Terry stayed with the kids. When we returned, Terry didn't say much about what we had purchased except when he noticed the two chandeliers with colorful lights. One of them was later put above the staircase leading up to the bedrooms in our new home. It was designed to play music and flash its lights on and off like in the dance scenes from the John Travolta film *Saturday Night Fever*. I replaced the strobe lights with regular, non-strobing bulbs and decided we could do without the music. Terry was happy.

After the air conditioners were installed, we decided to move into our new condominium. When we left the older apartment, I gave my brothers and sisters all the old furnishings, and they were happy to get them. My nephew Paul had a friend who owned a large truck that we used for moving various items to my siblings' homes. When they came to pick up everything, some of my family brought their children. When the adults started to load the truck, I handed out one dollar Ringgit bills to the children.

The truck driver saw this and said, "You hand out money as if it were leaves."

I smiled and said, "Yes, money grows on trees in America! Didn't you know that?" I paid him well for the use of his truck, and after the apartment had been cleaned out, I asked Juliana to sell it for me. It took a while, but several years later, someone finally purchased it-- after the landlord evicted the crazy troublemaker. As it turned out, we made a nice profit.

It was customary to have a priest come and give a blessing for a new home, so we did that after we were all set up in the condo. Afterward, we had a fantastic party. I arranged for a caterer to come and set up the food in front of our new home. When she asked me how many people to plan for, I told her at least a hundred. I called or otherwise got the word out to all my old friends to come and join us. I also told them to bring along a friend if they wanted to do so. And then, of course, there was my extended family. In the end, well over one hundred people came to the party. I couldn't blame them. It's hard to turn down free food and beer. I was delighted, and very happy that everyone came to our housewarming.

On the night of the blessing, the priest, who spoke reasonably good English, asked Terry a question if he would be kind enough to read a relatively long prayer before the party could begin. This was not something Terry wanted to do. He was not fond of speaking in public, and I wasn't eager to read it myself, because I feared I might have difficulty with some of the words. I began to think we might have a real problem.

Then, our granddaughter, Jadyn, spoke up and said she would be happy to read the prayer, and she did a great job! Both Terry and I were relieved. I gave the priest a donation, which was the custom, and he helped himself to a beer, and then the party began and lasted into the wee hours of the morning. And as far as I could tell, everyone enjoyed themselves and had a good time.

The following day, Terry, I, our daughter, and our grandkids all slept in, then got up and cleaned the living room of all traces of the party's detritus. We relaxed for the rest of the day, and when I saw the kids trying to find some program on the TV in English, I chuckled to myself but said nothing.

We, however, had to make plans for things to do because time was running short, and Aling would soon have to get back to her job in the states.

Terry and I would stay on for a few weeks longer. The first place we went to was Damai beach resort, a short drive from Kuching. We hadn't done this before, because we either were on a tight schedule, Terry was laid up, or we didn't have much money to spend. We had a nice, relaxed time, and enjoyed each other's company while basking in the sunshine on the beach.

There was another place I wanted to visit, specifically with Aling and her children. That place was Kampong Garung, where my father and mother had raised Aling as a child while I worked in Kuching to support them. Every few weeks, I would take the bus back to bring rice, money, and clothes for Aling to wear.

The following morning, we drove to Kampong Garung, where Aling and I had lived as a child. When we arrived, her children didn't have much to say, mainly because of the vast difference between the places they knew in the U.S.--Chicago and Tucson-- and where their mother and I had grown up. We weaved through the narrow dirt walkways between one hut or shanty after another. Then we walked down a hill where we saw my father's house atop another more extensive building.

It sat worn down and bleak, vacant for years even though we had built an extension in which my brothers would never live. Opening the unlocked wooden front door, we went inside. Still standing against the wall, the large wooden cabinet we both remembered appeared dank and rotting away. I looked at Terry and said, "Come on, let's take it outside and break it up for kindling."

As we pulled it away from the wall, we turned it to get it through the door. I noticed something hanging from a small hook by a cord on the back of the cabinet, something I recognized from long ago.

I gasped, breathless, and fell limp as tears welled up in my eyes. It had belonged to my grandfather; it was his headhunter's antique steel machete in its intricately designed leather sheath. I lifted it with care from the small hook on the back of the cabinet and held it close to my chest. I stood there, slowly breathing in and out as though I held my grandfather in a loving embrace. I looked at Terry, and he understood what we needed to do. We pushed the cabinet back against the wall, where it deserved to be, spared for guarding my grandfather's treasured trophy.

How did it get there? Perhaps my grandfather had hidden it there, safe and protected from the inevitable decay of the passing of time. Will I ever know? Probably not. But I am its keeper now. Today it hangs on our living room wall in Green Valley, a cherished memory of my early days with my grandfather.

It was a long drive back to Kuching. The traffic was heavy. I watched my lush, green jungle pass by as my eyes began to fill with tears. I wanted to cry but didn't. Emotions filled my heart as the car moved silently and in slow motion.

Next, we needed to decide what to do with Aling and her children; time was short now. With the discovery of my grandfather's machete, something inside me had clicked; my past had finally caught up with the present moment. Aling and her children would fly back to the States in a few days. And with the discovery of my grandfather's machete, something inside me had clicked; my past had finally caught up with the present moment. Since they had to fly through Kuala Lumpur, we would follow along with her and her kids.

It was time for us to reminisce. Aling had wanted to show her children where she had lived as a young teen after being adopted by my husband. And now, I wanted to show her where her father and I first met after we were married. Aling looked up the Malayan Hotel on the internet when the plane landed, but she could not find it. However, we stayed close to where it had been, at the Melia, a high-end hotel which turned out to be quite lovely.

The following morning, we found a taxi driver who remembered the Malayan. He took us there and stopped the car in front of an old soot-covered and sizeable vacant building. Surprisingly, the sign was still visible, red with white letters, still there, covered by time, but still unquestionably readable: "Malayan Hotel," it read.

I thought, "Time passes so fast, while we just go on living." Then we crossed the street where my husband and I had our wedding lunch. The place was still there but highly modified from what I remembered. I am sure the garcon, the old waiter we had nicknamed, was long dead. Terry and I raised our glasses to the good old days and times and fond memories. The following day, we took the train to Menara Sputeh and to the place of my husband's failed attempt to get Dr. Jack's herbal business off the ground. Now, memory lane was coming close to the end. Aling left Kuala Lumpur headed for home with the kids in tow. It had been a great adventure for them.

We flew back to Kuching, stayed for a few more days, and then headed back to Green Valley. I was in deep thought during the long flights, reflecting on my memories and roots. We made it home unscathed and were soon back to work, back to normal, and back to doing our job in the body shop.

As the days passed by one after the other, it was almost as if we hadn't been away. And then, something changed in me, and I felt a distinct sense of satisfaction and contentment. After work, one pleasant evening, my husband sat outside at our patio table, sipping his beer, as a glass of red wine sat on the table waiting for me. I could feel him watching me as I did my gardening. I like it when he does that. It gives me a sense of safety. As I transplanted a mum into a larger pot, I gently nursed the flower from its smaller home into its larger one because it had flourished and outgrown the bounds of the smaller pot. Then I stopped to look at its healthy roots. I smiled. They reminded me of our roots.

Twenty-nine years ago, Terry and I discovered each other merely by a chance meeting. Our roots then needed nurturing, as did the mum's roots I held before me. Over the years, Terry and I have learned to grow together. After all these years, our roots have become tangled tight by growth, and our love for one another has blossomed.

Above is a picture of Terry and Pedo in the backyard of their Green Valley home. Terry wears a T-shirt he made many years ago, showing a younger-looking Pedo. He is holding the actual sheath in which Pedo's grandfather carried his machete. Pedo holds the machete in her left hand, and in her right hand, she holds the only picture ever taken of her grandfather. (photo taken by Terry and Pedo's friend Jeff Babcock)

Thank you for exploring the ups and downs and unexpected journeys in my life, as I've experienced them. It means so much for me to be able to share my story with others and the lessons I have taken with me throughout my life. May you also never forget where you came from and be blessed to follow where life will take you. Terima kasih.

Pedo Rupa

www.ingramcontent.com/pod-product-compliance
Lightning Source LLC
LaVergne TN
LVHW010217070526
838199LV00062B/4635